25 YEARS OF LIFE-CHANGING MUSIC

25 *for* 25

PHILLIPS, CRAIG & DEAN

LEAFWOOD
PUBLISHERS
an imprint of Abilene Christian University Press

25 for 25
25 Years of Life-Changing Music

L E A F W O O D
P   U   B   L   I   S   H   E   R   S
an imprint of Abilene Christian University Press

Copyright © 2017 by Phillips, Craig & Dean

ISBN 978-0-89112-427-6 | LCCN 2017003432

Printed in the United States of America

Published in association with Mike Atkins Entertainment, 256 Seaboard Lane, Suite C-102, Franklin, TN 37067.

LIBRARY OF CONGRESS CATALOGING-IN-PUBLICATION DATA
Names: Phillips, Craig & Dean.
Title: 25 for 25 : 25 years of life-changing music / Phillips, Craig & Dean.
Other titles: Twenty-five for twenty-five
Description: Abilene, Texas : Leafwood Publishers, 2017.
Identifiers: LCCN 2017003432 | ISBN 9780891126027 (pbk.)
Subjects: LCSH: Phillips, Craig & Dean. | Contemporary Christian music—Texts.
Classification: LCC ML421.P53 P55 2017 | DDC 782.27092/2—dc23
LC record available at https://lccn.loc.gov/2017003432

Cover design by Thinkpen Design, LLC | Interior text design by Strong Design

Leafwood Publishers is an imprint of Abilene Christian University Press
ACU Box 29138
Abilene, Texas 79699

1-877-816-4455 | www.leafwoodpublishers.com

17 18 19 20 21 22 / 7 6 5 4 3 2 1

CONTENTS

25 Top Songs from 25 Years

Will You Love Jesus More?

TWENTY-FIVE YEARS AGO, WE SAT IN A NASHVILLE restaurant, sure that we had forever blown our shot at a recording deal. We had just finished a ten-song concert that was, in essence, a tryout for a record deal—and we had bombed, or so we thought.

Star Song had brought Randy to Music City a few months earlier to hear his solo record. He met with the marketing department. They informed him that they had too many male soloists. They asked if he would be interested in forming a group.

That's when Randy brought the three of us together. We had known each other for years. Growing up in similar church traditions, we knew each other from camps and other events. We had sung and led worship at each other's churches. But we never had actually sung together.

With each of us contributing a song and five thousand dollars, we got together in Dallas to produce a demo tape.

The record company must have liked what they heard, because they called later to ask if we could come to Nashville to play a concert. But we had a problem. We had only three songs, and we needed ten. We rushed to put together seven more songs and prepare for the Nashville concert.

That's when we had that epic collapse. Much to our surprise, though, two weeks after the concert, Star Song called and asked us to make an album with them.

It hardly seems possible that was twenty-five years ago. At that time, we wouldn't have dared to dream that the Lord would use our music the way he has. We just wanted to use the gifts he gave us to serve him. When we put together that three-song demo tape in Dallas, we thought that might be the only music we'd ever create together.

Yet God had other plans.

We feel incredibly privileged that those plans have included you. We're grateful that over the past quarter century you have allowed us to share some of the special moments of your life. Whether you played "Shine On Us" at your wedding, or pulled over on the side of the road the first time you heard "I Want to Be Just Like You," or you played "Midnight Oil" at your mother's funeral, it has been a privilege to share a significant section of this road with you.

When we see you at a concert, listen to you sing our songs, and hear the stories of how God has used the songs in your life, it does as much for us—as we pray it is doing for you. We have enjoyed the opportunity to worship the Lord together with you.

Even as our music styles (and hair styles!) have changed, your support has remained remarkably consistent. You may have enjoyed our harmonies, but we also believe you've stuck with us because you appreciate the honesty in the songs we've written—along with our unflinching desire and determination to reflect the gospel of grace.

As much as we appreciate all the encouragement you've given to us throughout the years, we hope and pray that our music hasn't lifted us up in your eyes. The prayer that drives our ministry today—as it has for twenty-five years—is best reflected in a song we recorded years ago.

Will you love Jesus more
When we go our separate ways
When this moment is a memory
Will you remember His face
Will you look back and realize
You sensed His love more than you did before
I pray for nothing less
Than for you to love Jesus more

If we've done that during the past twenty-five years, we've been true to what God has called us to do.

—Randy Phillips, Shawn Craig, and Dan Dean

Revelation Song

Composed by Jennie Lee Riddle
Album: *Fearless* (2009)

"Holy, holy, holy is the Lord God Almighty, who was, and is, and is to come. . . . You are worthy, our Lord and God, to receive glory and honor and power, for you created all things, and by your will they were created and have their being." (Rev. 4:8, 11 NIV)

Worthy is the,
Lamb who was slain
Holy, Holy, is He
Sing a new song, to Him who sits on
Heaven's Mercy Seat
Repeat 2x

Chorus:
Holy, Holy, Holy
Is the Lord God Almighty
Who was, and is, and is to come
With all creation I sing:

Praise to the King of Kings!
You are my everything,
And I will adore You . . !

Yeah!

Clothed in rainbows, of living color
Flashes of lightning, rolls of thunder
Blessing and honor, strength and
Glory and power be
To You the Only Wise King,
Yeah

Repeat Chorus:

Filled with wonder,
Awestruck wonder
At the mention of Your Name
Jesus, Your Name is Power
Breath, and Living Water
Such a marvelous mystery
Yeah . . .

Chorus:
Holy, Holy, Holy
Is the Lord God Almighty
Who was, and is, and is to come,
With all creation I sing:
Praise to the King of Kings!

You are my everything,

And—I—will—adore YOU . . .

Chorus (Repeat a cappella)

GMA Dove Award—Inspirational Album of the Year, 2010

The Story Behind the Song

Long before we recorded "Revelation Song," it was a favorite
of ours. We led our congregations in singing it for years,
and it always seemed to take people to the throne of God.

Still, it never dawned on us that we should put it on
an album. For one thing, we wouldn't be the first to cover
it. It had already appeared on Kari Jobe's first album, and
several other great artists had done it as well.

Then came the God-moment that changed our whole
perspective on the song. We included it with a number of
songs that we sang at the famed Brooklyn Tabernacle with
their Grammy-award-winning choir.

And God revealed himself that afternoon in a fresh way.

The curtains of Heaven opened, and God exposed our
hearts to an external glimpse of what Heaven would look

like with Jesus sitting on the throne. In that moment, we each had trouble singing. We even had trouble breathing. It was such a holy, unforgettable moment—the kind of moment that changes you.

We never looked at "Revelation Song" the same way again. Conventional wisdom said we shouldn't fill a spot on our upcoming "Fearless" album with a song that had been done so many times before. We needed to save spots for new songs.

Yet that song wouldn't leave our heads—or hearts.

God's hand seemed to be on us every time we sang it. Our record label didn't understand or agree without fervor, but we insisted that it be included on the album.

Another moment that really made it clear to us that God would use this song came not long after we released it. We were doing a number of free, "brown bag" concerts that were sponsored by radio stations on a first-come, first-serve basis. Before one particular concert, the venue, which held thousands, filled to capacity, and hundreds of people were turned away. We couldn't help but wonder, *Are they really here to see us?*

As we began the intro to "Revelation Song," we felt like we were experiencing a little bit of Heaven. Dan started the first part of the song, and people started singing along—thousands of people on their feet—and we saw then that there was something very special about this song.

At that moment we realized this song was bigger than us—and it really was. Every once in a while, you have a moment when you realize you are witnessing God touching people in a special way. That night, with "Revelation Song" in the air, it became all about Jesus, not about Phillips, Craig & Dean. And after that night, God showed up every time we sang "Revelation Song."

Still, we didn't hold out any hope for the song to become a radio hit. It had been covered by just too many other talented artists. In fact, one day as we were finishing up on the tracking, the record's producer, Bernie Herms, asked for some input on how to end the song.

"Bernie, it doesn't really matter," Dan told him. "Do a fade. Do whatever you want with this song. It will never see the light of day on the radio."

But it did. Dan Michaels, our radio representative, listened to the album, trying to figure out which songs would be best to release as singles. When he listened to "Revelation Song," God did a work on his heart. He was certain that it had to be our first release to radio.

"Revelation Song" spent more time at Number One than any other Christian song that year. Looking back, the song's appeal probably shouldn't have surprised us. It hits an immediate need in our lives.

Too many times today, we look for security in all the wrong places—and doing that will always leave us anxious.

Instead, the Bible tells us to find security by looking to the greatness and majesty of God.

That's exactly what this song encourages us to do. It captures a moment of worship—when we look up into Heaven, peel back the curtain of eternity, and glimpse what awaits us there. Everything else fades away as we join the saints singing, "Holy, holy, holy is the Lord God Almighty, who was, and is, and is to come" (Rev. 4:8 NIV).

For a brief moment, we experienced this when we sang "Revelation Song" in Brooklyn that night. It has been such a privilege to help others do the same ever since. **—Randy, Shawn, & Dan**

I love "Revelation Song." It's a song we've sung at church many times. As a group, we had talked about trying to cover the song at the right time. We felt passionate about it. When I hear that song, whatever circumstance I'm in, it takes me to that place. And where is that place? It's in the presence of Jesus Christ. **—Randy Phillips**

It's not just the lyrics, and it's not just the music. It's the combination of all of it together that takes you on a journey. It lifts your spirit. I've seen it happen many times in our church as we do the song in worship, and it's always an amazing thing to witness. "Revelation Song," is definitely a song that transports people to a place in Christ that only a song like this can do. **—Dan Dean**

In uncertain times, it's easy for us to focus on the things that we're afraid of and in a sense to magnify whatever it is that we're going through. The Bible says, "O magnify the LORD with me, and let us exalt his name together" (Ps. 34:3 KJV). What I love about "Revelation Song" is that it captures that idea. The unique thing about God is that when you magnify him, instead of seeing flaws, as you and I do when we look in a magnifying glass, we actually see the greatness of God. We see the longsuffering, the mercy, the gentleness of our Lord. That's why this song is so awesome. It magnifies the person of Christ, who is worthy to be praised. **—Shawn Craig**

Lessons from "Revelation Song"

Randy, Shawn & Dan say, "Too many times today, we look for security in all the wrong places—and that will always leave you nervous. Instead, the Bible tells us to find security by looking to the awesomeness of God." Where do you look for security? If it's not God, why? What will it take for you to find total security in him?

_____

_____

_____

_____

_____

_____

_____

_____

_____

_____

_____

_____

_____

_____

Read this as a praise prayer to God—

> Holy, Holy, Holy is the Lord God Almighty Who was,
> and is, and is to come
> With all creation I sing: Praise to the King of Kings!
> You are my everything, And I will adore You . . . !
>
> Blessing and honor, strength and Glory and power be
> to You the only wise King. I'm filled with wonder at the
> mention of Your Name
>
> Holy, Holy, Holy is the Lord God Almighty Who was,
> and is, and is to come,
> Come lift up his Name, the King of Kings . . .We will adore
> You, Lord . . .
> King of heaven and earth, King Jesus
>
> Hallelujah, Hallelujah, Hallelujah!
> Majesty, honor and power and strength and dominion
> To You Lord, to the King of Glory
>
> "Worthy is the Lamb, who was slain, to receive power and
> wealth and wisdom and strength and honor and glory
> and praise! To him who sits on the throne and to the
> Lamb be praise and honor and glory and power, for ever
> and ever!" (Rev. 5:12–13 NIV).

Revelation Song: *Testimonies*

"This is God's word, set to song. In this most recent time in the wilderness, it has been medicine to my soul." —Buddy Davis

"LOVE THIS ALBUM!! Every song gets to my heart. I have had days that I have just left it on repeat. Uplifting, beautiful, drawing you closer to the LORD. Wonderful worship music." —Anonymous

"Fantastic music as always from these guys. They will never cease to bring me closer to the Lord with their music. If anyone knows how to do it, it would be these guys who have been worshiping through their music for a very long time." —Brian Looney

"We love their music, and their stand for Christ, especially in a world where it is not a popular stand to take. They do a lot of great music on this CD, but the best and most powerful, I think, is their rendition of 'The Revelation Song.' Wow! It knocks my socks off every time I hear it! This is really a powerful song!

"Now, my husband and our 16-year-old son, are both listening to it now, and really enjoying it! We love it because it is more than just music, but as they worship the Lord through their music, they cause us to do the same." —Carol Lugg

"[These] three men sharing the Word of God is a strong message for the world." —Anonymous

"I almost cry each time I play the Revelation song (Rev. 4) because it reminds me of 'home.'" —Anonymous

"Love this song! My kids call it the holy, holy, holy song. Makes me smile when they ask to hear it." —TruBluize

Jennie Lee Riddle, Songwriter, "Revelation Song"

I actually wrote the song in response to a decade-long prayer that came out of another song that said, "I see men from every nation bowing down before the throne." The first time I heard that song, I knew that he had written it out of what he foresaw, and it had become my earnest prayer to see it become a reality in my lifetime.

And I prayed constantly that Jesus would raise up one bride to lift up one voice to one King. The worship songs at that time were more prayer-oriented, and there was a lot of "I" and "me" in them, acknowledging just us. I was at a point where I thought, "I have enough of me." And I felt like the whole Church kind of had too.

We needed someone so much bigger than ourselves and to lift our eyes up off of our daily lives and off of the rubble and off of the worry and magnify him.

I never had any idea that it would travel like it has and bless as many people as it has. It's such a dear and precious thing, because God is letting me see my prayer come true. I've asked him that we would all get to see one bride come together and lift one voice to one King. To get to see every generation, every denomination, every nationality singing to him and enjoying his beauty and his holiness and him wrapping her up as one has been just overwhelming and humbling. **—Jennie Lee Riddle**

Great Are You Lord

Composed by James Rueger and Tony Wood
Album: *Fearless* (2009)

*"We give thanks to you, Lord God Almighty, the One
who is and who was, because you have taken your
great power and have begun to reign." (Rev. 11:17 NIV)*

The beauty of Your majesty
Displayed for all the world to see
Is it any wonder
Is it any wonder

The glory of your holiness
The mercy of your faithfulness
Is it any wonder
Is it any wonder
(And) We sing

Chorus:
Great are You Lord
For we adore You
Lift up Your name

And fall before You
We stand in awe
And sing great are You Lord
We lift up our voice
We sing holy, holy
Hallelujah
To the one and only
Forevermore
We'll sing great are You Lord

Through endless ages You will reign
Yet every season you're the same
Is it any wonder
Is it any wonder

Your power of Your redeeming plan
The grace that offers life to man
Is it any wonder
Is it any wonder
(And) We sing

GMA Dove Award—Inspirational Album of the Year, 2010

The Story Behind the Song

When you pull back the curtain of a musician's work, you'll often discover it isn't as easy as it seems. You hear the finished product. We hear the not-so-finished product.

"Great Are You Lord" was one of those songs that wasn't easy to record—particularly for Dan and Shawn. As Bernie Herms, our producer on the album, pushed us to demonstrate the kind of energy the chorus required, Shawn and Dan, who were singing the higher parts, had to keep taking the vocals up a notch.

It took us just about a full day to hash out the song. We thought that day would never end.

But the day of hard work was well worth it. We love vertical songs like this one that exalt the Name of Jesus and speak directly to the greatness of God. We can either choose to sing about the greatness of God—or sing directly to him about his greatness. We prefer the latter.

When you've been putting together records for twenty-five years, it's easy to lose focus on what really matters when making music—especially when you've seen a level of success. It's easy to make much of your music and much of yourself. Even Christian artists can fall into this trap.

Songs like "Great Are You Lord" bring you back to your senses. As James Rueger and Tony Wood penned these words, they echoed themes that men like Isaiah and David wrote thousands of years earlier.

Through Isaiah, God says:
To whom then will you compare me,
that I should be like him? says the Holy One.
Lift up your eyes on high and see:
who created these?
He who brings out their host by number,
calling them all by name,
by the greatness of his might,
and because he is strong in power
not one is missing. (Isa. 40:25–26 NIV)

No one compares to the Lord. No matter how many points the best basketball, football, or baseball player in the world scores, no matter how many albums the most celebrated artist of the age sells, no matter how much earthly power a political leader has, none of them can even begin to compare with who God is. He excels in every area.

We need to hear that. We need to revel in the Lord's greatness. Only then can we discover who we were made to be.

We all have everyday problems that threaten to pull our focus off of God. When we magnify the Lord—literally make him bigger in our lives—everything else gets smaller. The pain, relational struggles, and frustrations all pale in comparison to a magnified Jesus.

And that's the life we were born to live.—**Randy, Shawn & Dan**

Lessons from "Great Are You Lord"

Randy, Shawn & Dan say, "No one compares to who God is. We need to hear that. We need to revel in his greatness. Only then can we discover who we were made to be." How will your life be different now that you know that the only way you can discover who you really are is to embrace the greatness of God?

_____

_____

_____

_____

_____

Randy, Shawn & Dan say, "We all have everyday problems that threaten to pull our focus off of God. When we magnify the Lord—literally make him bigger in our lives—everything else gets smaller. And that's the life we were born to live." What are the things that pull your focus off God? How can you keep your focus on God?

_____

_____

_____

_____

_____

Mediate on this verse: "'To whom will you compare me?
Or who is my equal?' says the Holy One. Lift your eyes and
look to the heavens: Who created all these? He who brings
out the starry host one by one, and calls them each by name.
Because of his great power and mighty strength, not one of
them is missing" (Isa. 40:25–26 NIV).

_____

_____

_____

_____

_____

What is God telling you about this verse? How might it
apply to your life?

_____

_____

_____

_____

_____

Throne of Praise

With our actions, our words, and our worship, we create a place of honor for God to sit and dwell. We've all witnessed this in our churches on a Sunday. It's not about the building, or the place where we come together, or the day of the week; it's about when God's people come together and, in a spirit of community, begin to lift him and exalt him. Although Revelation tells us he already has a throne he dwells on, with our worship, we create this place for him to come and sit with us, and it's a place of reverence and respect and honor. **—Dan Dean**

When the Stars Burn Down (Blessing & Honor)

Composed by Jennie Lee Riddle and Jonathan Lee
Album: Breathe In (2012)

"*And every creature which is in heaven and on the
earth and under the earth and such as are in the sea,
and all that are in them, I heard saying:*

> '*Blessing and honor and glory and power
> Be to Him who sits on the throne,
> And to the Lamb, forever and ever!*'" (Rev. 5:13 NKJV)

When the stars burn down and the earth wears out
and we stand before the throne,
With the witnesses who have gone before,
We will rise and all applaud.

Singing, "Blessing and honor and glory and power
forever to our God." [*2x*]

When the hands of time wind fully down
And the earth is rolled up like a scroll,
The trumpets will call and the world will fall to its knees
as we go home.

Singing, "Blessing and honor and glory and power forever to our God." [*4x*]

Star of the morning
Light of salvation
Majesty

God of all mysteries
Lord of the universe
Righteous king
Repeat]
There will come a day, standing face to face, in a moment we'll be like Him.
He will wipe our eyes dry and take us up to His side
And forever we will be His.

Singing, "Blessing and honor and glory and power forever to our God." [repeat]
Oh, oh, oh, oh

Forever to our God
Oh, oh, oh, oh

The Story Behind the Song

When you write a song like "Revelation Song," you get plenty of artists knocking on your door wanting to perform your songs. I'm sure that was the case for Jennie Riddle. We sure wanted to work with Jennie again after our relationship began with "Revelation Song."

That's why when we first started hearing from people at Gateway Church in Dallas about a new song by Jennie that they were singing in their worship services, we were all ears. Jenny then told us that while she'll never write another "Revelation Song," this song had many of the same elements—particularly a passionate focus on the ultimate revelation, Jesus

The song really lays out a powerful scene about the destiny of everything God has made.

> When the stars burn down and the earth wears out
> and we stand before the throne,
> With the witnesses who have gone before,
> We will rise and all applaud.
>
> Singing, "Blessing and honor and glory and
> power forever to our God."

Those words echoed the verse in 2 Peter, "The day of the Lord will come like a thief. The heavens will disappear with a roar; the elements will be destroyed by fire, and the earth and everything done in it will be laid bare" (3:10).

One day there will be an end to this world we're living in. Writers have said before that one day this world will "fold up like a tent," once God is done with this world and his redemptive story is done in Jesus Christ.

Everything you see, everything you touch, everything you smell, everything you taste, and everything you feel has been created for the glory of God. Once that purpose has been completed, it will be no more—and Jesus will get every bit of glory due him.

We can't wait for that day to come. **—Randy, Shawn & Dan**

This is one of those epic worship songs that is similar to "Revelation Song." In fact the same writer wrote both songs. When I first heard "When the Stars Burn Down," it immediately had the same impact of "Revelation Song," with that big worship moment where you're transported out of this mortal world and into the next world. **—Randy Phillips**

It's a song that puts things into perspective; it reminds us what life is really all about. We have only a brief moment to experience this life, and this thing we call time is going to be over so soon. It's not what we are ultimately created for, but, nonetheless, there is great purpose for our time here. **—Dan Dean**

This song encompasses the idea of the unveiling of Jesus Christ in his glory and the melting down of the universe. When all of that is said and done, when the universe folds up like a tent, Jesus Christ is still King, still Lord. Jesus is still shining. **—Shawn Craig**

About the *Breathe In* album—

There are so many people walking around in the world today who are breathing, but they're not alive. This album, *Breathe In,* is about that. Breathe in. Start experiencing life on the scale that God wants you to. **—Dan Dean**

Breathe In is just about taking a big breath of oxygen. It seems like people are so deflated spiritually, deflated mentally, deflated in their hope. Through this album we hope to say, breathe in. Take a deep breath of God, and let it expand your soul and bring you hope, and let God deposit something heavenly in your earthen vessel.

Breathe In is about experiencing the hope of God again. **—Randy Phillips**

Lessons from "When the Stars Burn Down"

The Bible says, "He will swallow up death forever. The Lord God will wipe away all tears and take away forever all insults and mockery against his land and people. The Lord has spoken—he will surely do it!" (Isa. 25:8 TLB). If you deeply, deeply believed this, how would your life change?

_____

_____

_____

_____

_____

_____

_____

Meditate on the Scripture passage—"The Lord is not slow in keeping his promise, as some understand slowness. He is patient with you, not wanting anyone to perish, but everyone to come to repentance.

"But the day of the Lord will come like a thief. The heavens will disappear with a roar; the elements will be destroyed by fire, and the earth and everything in it will be laid bare" (2 Pet. 3:9–10 NIV).

_____

_____

_____

_____

_____

_____

_____

What is God telling you about this passage? How might it apply to your life?

_____

_____

_____

_____

_____

_____

When the Stars Burn Down:
Testimonies

"I listen to this song in my car on my daily commute to work, but I really love to listen to it at home; there I can worship the Lord and really hear what this song is about." —Cathy N

"Some Christian artists depart from scripture so far that you can't really find their tenuous connection to the Word, but that's not the case with [Phillips, Craig & Dean]. I love the references in this song to the triumphant return of Jesus: 'The trumpets will call and the world will fall to its knees as we all go home . . .' With scriptural lyrics taken from John the Beloved's Book of Revelation and also from Isaiah, this song is one that will really lift you up. Jesus truly is our righteous King who will comfort those who mourn and wipe away our tears. This God is our God forever and ever! You will want to sing along with the refrain: 'Blessing, honor, and glory, and power forever to our God!'" —apriles78

"This song helps remind all Christians that God is in control of EVERYTHING!! Hopefully this song will also peak the interest of non-believers." —Modello

"Man, I love this song! Extremely powerful, prophetic and moving. I played it at my dad's funeral and there was not a dry eye in the house." —Gene

Jesus, Only Jesus

Composed by Chris Tomlin, Christy Nockels, Kristian
Stanfill, Matt Redman, Nathan Nockels, and Tony Wood
Album: *Above It All* (2014)

*"Therefore God exalted him to the highest place and
gave him the name that is above every name, that at
the name of Jesus every knee should bow, in heaven
and on earth and under the earth, and every tongue
confess that Jesus Christ is Lord, to the glory of God
the Father." (Phil. 2:9–11 NIV)*

Who has the power to raise the dead?
Who can save us from our sin?
He is our hope, our righteousness
Jesus, only Jesus

Who can make the blind to see?
Who holds the keys that set us free?
He paid it all to bring us peace
Jesus, only Jesus

Holy, King almighty Lord
Saints and angels all adore
I join with them and bow before
Jesus, only Jesus

Who can command the highest praise?
Who has the name above all names?
You stand alone, I stand amazed
Jesus, only Jesus

You will command the highest praise!
Yours is the name above all names!
You stand alone, I stand amazed
Jesus, only Jesus!
Jesus, only Jesus!

The Story Behind the Song

You've probably heard athletes talk about certain days where they just can't miss. Everything slows down around them. It's not that they've done anything particularly right—rather, it's a gift. As followers of Christ, we realize it's just a moment of grace.

That's what happened to me when we recorded "Jesus, Only Jesus." It should have been a tough song. It was the first song we recorded for the *Fearless* album. Since it was pitched high, I knew Nathan Nockels, our producer, would be trying to do the same thing most producers do with similar songs. Get whoever is singing the lead vocals (which was me for this song) to take it up a notch in order to bring the energy. I had no idea how I'd do it.

But God came through. I've never had a vocal performance quite like that. Nathan pulled out of me just the right vocals for the song. I nailed it as well as I ever have for a song. There are notes in the vocal that require me to go to the top of my range, and to my surprise, I hit them easily.

Nathan had a good day, too, but it wasn't about his performance or mine. Truly, I think, it was Jesus, Only Jesus. The recording became a great metaphor for what this song is all about.

As lead pastors of different churches, we have a wide spectrum of issues that greet us each week—from people facing physical sickness to suicide to abandonment.

Then you look at the needs in our communities, and those are just multiplied. None of us have all the tools necessary to minister to all of the brokenness around us. Nobody does. Sometimes the prayer requests that come in simply overwhelm us.

None of us have the ability to be right on target with our ministry on our own.

Yet we're thankful we can point them to a real answer —"Jesus, Only Jesus." We don't have the answers, but we know he does. We don't need the ability to hit every right note. We know he has all the ability in the world to create all the right notes. He is the Alpha and Omega—the First and the Last. Nothing escapes his understanding.

> Who can make the blind to see?
> Who holds the keys that set us free?
> He paid it all to bring us peace
> Jesus, only Jesus

"That's why this song has resonated so much with us. It makes much of Jesus, and reminds us that, at the end of the day, nothing matters more than him." **—Dan**

"Jesus, Only Jesus resonates with the three of us as pastors. We have congregants that come to us often and want us to help them with their challenges in life. Some of these challenges are so complicated, I find myself often thinking, *I have no way to help you.* I don't know what to point you to. Counseling is great, but sometimes people hit a place where the only thing you can point them to is Jesus, only Jesus. The great thing about that is he can breathe hope into you for the season of life you're in and take you to a place of healing." **—Randy**

Lessons from "Jesus, Only Jesus"

The Bible says, "'I am the Alpha and the Omega,' says the Lord God, 'who is, and who was, and who is to come, the Almighty'" (Rev. 1:8 NIV). Our Lord God is the Beginning and the End. What does the fact that God is the same yesterday, today, and tomorrow mean in your life? What does that mean about your past, present, and future?

_____

_____

_____

_____

_____

_____

_____

The song lyrics say, "Who has the power to raise the dead? Who can save us from our sin? He is our hope, our righteousness, Jesus, only Jesus." If God has the power to raise the dead, then he has the power to do what in your life? What can God resurrect in your life?

_____

_____

_____

_____

_____

_____

_____

_____

The Bible says, "For I resolved to know nothing while I was with you except Jesus Christ and him crucified" (1 Cor. 2:2NIV). What might happen if you made this a New Year's resolution?

_____

_____

_____

_____

_____

_____

_____

_____

Jesus, Only Jesus: *Testimonies*

"Awesome praise and worship song! Really gets you moving and ready to start worshiping Jesus Christ!" —Kathleen M

"Though I'm more of a Christian Rock and Gospel Hip Hop Fan, these old dudes as I call them, really bring it. The lyrics. The melodies. The way they sing their songs with meaning and purpose, I always keep them in my iPod with guys like Lecrae, Tobymac, Crowder, and Kutless." —Michael H

"Listening to it brings visions of what it would be like for the entire heavenly body to be singing. It has such a calming effect as it puts you in the presence of the Lord Almighty." —James S

"Phillips, Craig & Dean's theological, holy and reverent style of writing and singing worship songs has consistently attracted me. You'll quickly be singing the reverent chorus: 'Holy, King Almighty Lord, saints and angels all adore, I'll join with them and bow before Jesus, Only Jesus.'" —Kevin D

Why We're Committed to the Local Church

For us, serving in ministry in a local church in addition to our work through Phillips, Craig & Dean has always been a passion for each of us. We get to do two things we dearly love. We have never felt like we've had to give up anything.

We and the record company were thrown off guard by the success of our first album. Record company executives asked us to quit our ministerial positions, move to Nashville, and get serious about our music. But the three of us were in complete agreement. That wasn't something we were prepared to do. We'll continue to do both for as long as God allows.

One spills over into another. What happens at the church spills over into our writing. Our songs have been birthed in the church.

That's been our legacy for twenty-five years. **—Randy**

When we first got started, Randy was serving as an administrative pastor at a church in Austin. Shawn and I were both worship leaders. We had a conversation where we asked one another what we would do if Phillips, Craig & Dean really took off. Would we continue to serve in our local churches? Because the local church had given birth to all the good that had come from our ministries, we decided we'd stay connected to our local churches—no matter what. Fortunately, the senior pastors we worked for saw God's hand in what was happening in our music ministry and were all willing to work with us. They allowed us to miss one Sunday a month as long as everything was covered.

A few years later we had another huge decision for our ministry. We began to go out on longer tours—thirty-to-forty-day tours. We had to decide once again whether we were willing to lessen our commitments to our local churches and miss more than one Sunday a month. Once again, we decided to remain firmly rooted in our home churches. We'd fly in on Sunday for church and fly back out on Monday.

We felt like the input and value of the local church was worth the sacrifice. At some point, we each became senior pastors and decided we would no longer perform on Saturday nights.

It has served us well. I think that commitment has paid off in a number of ways. For example, we didn't move to Nashville and do two hundred dates a year. Many groups burn out when they do that. They do so many dates just to survive. We have each always had a second source of income, so we didn't feel the same pressure to add dates to the calendar. Our music ministry remains a labor of love.

In addition, it has given us space as friends. When we're apart, we're apart. You've heard the saying, "Good fences make good neighbors." More than a fence, we've had miles and miles between us. I believe that has increased the longevity of our group—and our friendship. —**Dan**

Longtime faithfulness in ministry isn't very popular today. Too often, ministry leaders find themselves locked into a perpetual search for the next "big thing," the next great opportunity. But over and over, the ministry leaders we've served with at local churches have modeled long-term faithfulness before us. We've seen the fruit that God has grown from their faithfulness. Now God has led us to model that faithfulness in our ministries.

At the beginning of Rick Warren's ministry, he asked, "Lord, if I could, I'd like to give my life to one group of believers." That's always been my prayer too. We're not critical of others who make other choices. Maybe God has called them to do that. For us, just putting our hands to the plow and remaining steady and faithful have been their own reward.

It used to be easy to get an early flight on Sunday mornings, but it's not anymore. Since that has become true, we've had to limit our Saturday night concerts—which is a huge deal in the music industry. We think it's important to be in our home churches on as many Sundays as possible. It's not a hard-and-fast rule. There are times we make exceptions. We each miss about four weekends a year.

But we see the value of plugging in every Sunday. We're like batteries. Sure, we're full of the Spirit and Jesus lives in us, but "we leak." God has designed the spiritual life for us to "walk by the Spirit" and not just "live by the Spirit." We need to plug in on a regular basis. **—Shawn**

Great, Great God

Composed by David Moore
Album: *Breathe In* (2012)

"*I am the* LORD, *and there is no other; apart from me
there is no God. I will strengthen you, though you
have not acknowledged me, so that from the rising of
the sun to the place of its setting men may know there
is none besides me. I am the* LORD, *and there is no
other.*" (Isa. 45:5–6 NIV)

Your cross gave life
Hope and salvation
full restoration
promise for all
Your grace has made
us part of Your kingdom
living in freedom
heirs with Your son

Chorus
Jesus Your name
is alive

now Your redemption draws into our lives
strong in battle
You overcame
and the victory's ours
now we sing
Great, Great there is no one like our God
Great, Great there is no one like our God

Our walls fall down
strongholds are broken
eternity spoken
righteous we stand
the church will rise
declaring Your kingdom
shouting your freedom
blood of the Lamb

Chorus
Jesus Your name
is alive
now Your redemption draws into our lives
strong in battle
You overcame
and the victory's ours
now we sing
Great, Great there is no one like our God
Great, Great there is no one like our God

Great, Great there is no one like our God

Great, Great there is no one like our God

Bridge
You reign in all the earth
You reign victorious
Your power is limitless
There is no one like our God
no one like our God
yeaaa
Great, Great there is no one like our God
Great, Great there is no one like our God
Great, Great there is no one like our God
Great, Great there is no one like our God
No one like Our God

The Story Behind the Song

Clint lewis, a friend of ours at Gateway Church in Dallas, connected us with this song. He has been instrumental in helping us find several of our bestr songs, including "You Are God Alone" and "When the Stars Burn Down." This time, he brought us the work of David Moore, a young guy on Gateway's worship team. God obviously had his hand on this young man in a very profound way. It's hard to imagine such rich worship lyrics coming from someone so young. Clint knew we were recording and thought this would be a great fit for the album.

And it was.

One thing that makes it a particularly strong song for us is the echoing back and forth about the greatness of God. The audience participation makes it a powerful vehicle for lifting up the Name of Jesus together. We've had some sweet moments in concerts through this song.

The song describes God and his awesome goodness and power, and it seems like worshipers cannot sit still on the sideline. When they hear this song, they seem compelled to let their hearts express what God has already done for them. He is a great, great God.

Every time we sing the song we're reminded of verses like, "I am the LORD, and there is no other; apart from me there is no God. I will strengthen you, though you have not acknowledged me" (Isa. 45:5 NIV). Nothing compares to the Lord. His greatness is unmatched. His power is unequaled. His goodness is unparalleled. Truly, there is no one like our God. In the song we sing:

> You reign in all the earth
> You reign victorious

Your power is limitless
There is no one like our God
no one like our God

It's hard to forget the setting where we recorded the song. We were at Chris Tomlin's studio—an old, restored house in a country setting. Majestic trees were all around us. The Georgia sun shone brightly that day. The greatness of God was so evident in the nature that surrounded us that it made it easier to sing about the uniqueness of God's power and goodness.

One of the first times we sang the song live was during a special event at Gateway Church. We had just released the album, so it was great to perform something fresh. What made it a particularly memorable performance was that we got to sing the song with David, the writer, who is a big part of the church's worship band. He came up on stage and took the second verse of the song. When the Gateway Church audience saw him on the stage singing his song with us, they erupted. It was a terrific moment. **—Randy, Shawn & Dan**

One thing that we keep hearing throughout the lyrics is the greatness of God. As people hear songs like "Great, Great God," we hope that they might lift up their eyes and see God, and then maybe their problems will look a little smaller. **—Shawn Craig**

Lessons from "Great, Great God"

The song lyrics say, "Great, Great there is no one like our God." How does this lyric express the biblical truth that you can trust in God?

_____

_____

_____

_____

_____

_____

_____

_____

_____

If God's power is limitless, what does this tell you about his ability to help you, regardless of your circumstances?

_____

_____

_____

_____

_____

_____

_____

_____

_____

Based on Isaiah 40:28 (below), what are several character-
istics that make God Great?

_____

_____

_____

_____

_____

_____

_____

> "Do you not know? Have you not heard? The LORD
> is the everlasting God, the Creator of the ends of
> the earth. He will not grow tired or weary, and his
> understanding no one can fathom" (Isa. 40:28 NIV).

What Is God Like?
By Shawn Craig

That evening they brought to him many who were
oppressed by demons, and he cast out the spirits with
a word and healed all who were sick. (Matt. 8:16 ESV)

So what was he like? Was he friendly? Was he as funny as he seems? Those are the questions we ask when someone we know hangs out with someone famous. What we're asking is if the person they appear to be is the same person they are up close and personal. Because we know that for most, there is the person everyone sees and then there is the person that they really are. The public image doesn't always match the private one.

What is God like? Is he kind? Does he really care? What would it feel like to really talk to God, face to face? The closest we can come to the answers to these questions is found in one place—or more honestly, one Person. Namely, the One we read about here in Matthew 8 as we see most vividly in this verse:

> That evening they brought to him many who were
> oppressed by demons, and he cast out the spirits
> with a word and healed all who were sick. (8:16)

Do you want to know how God feels about those whose emotions and soul are captive to darkness? Look at what

Jesus did when he came face to face with these captives: "He cast out the spirits with a word."

How does God feel about those suffering physically? Consider his response to those who were sick: He healed "all who were sick."

God has revealed his kindness through the Scriptures, yes. But more powerfully than that, God has revealed it in a Person, his Son, Jesus. This Person shows us exactly what God is like: his care, his compassion, his character, his love.

So bring your questions to him today. Picture yourself before the One we read about in this passage. As Jesus is touching and healing with a word, present your questions there. We can rest our hearts in this picture painted for us in the Gospel—as we find here in Matthew, a tax collector who lived and walked with the love of God revealed—Jesus of Nazareth.

Prayer: *Father God, sometimes I wish I could talk with You face to face. I tremble at the thought, yet I wonder. Thank You for making Yourself known not only in Your precious word preserved for us, but most powerfully in the giving of Your Son, Jesus Christ who revealed to us Your kindness, care, and how much You really love me. So I wait here in Your Presence to know the width, length, depth, and height of Your love.*

Let My Words Be Few

Composed by Beth Redman and Matt Redman
Album: *Let My Words Be Few* (2001)

*"Who will not stand in awe of you, Lord? Who will
refuse to declare your greatness? You alone are holy.
All the nations will come and worship you, because
your just actions are seen by all." (Rev. 15:4 TEV)*

You are God in heaven
And here am I on earth
So I'll let my words be few
Jesus, I am so in love with You

And I'll stand in awe of You, Jesus
Yes, I'll stand in awe of You
And I'll let my words be few
Jesus, I am so in love with You

The simplest of all love songs
I want to bring to You, oh yeah
So I'll let my words be few, hey
Jesus, I am so in love with You

And I'll stand in awe of You, Jesus
Yes, I'll stand in awe of You
And I'll let my words be few
Jesus, I am so in love with You

You are God in heaven
And here am I on earth
So I'll let my words be few
Jesus, I am so in love with You

And I'll stand in awe of You, Jesus
Yes, I'll stand in awe of You
And I'll let my words be few
Jesus, I am so in love with You

And I'll stand in awe of You, Jesus
Yes, I'll stand in awe of You
And I'll let my words be few
Jesus, I am so in love with You

So in love with you, yeah
Jesus, hey, yeah

The Story Behind the Song

Typically, musicians are creatures of habit. We're no exception. That's why when we were in Minneapolis one time and a radio station asked us to visit with a fan before the concert, we were honestly a bit reluctant. But when we heard the man's story, we were eager to help.

Dying of cancer, the man had wanted to attend the concert as his last request—and he wanted to hear us sing one particular song. When we met with him and his family before the concert, we found out his favorite song was "Let My Words Be Few." His illness had robbed him of much of the ability to speak, but he held tightly to the biblical truth that God could understand the words of his heart even if he couldn't physically express them.

With the help of his family, he told us that "Let My Words Be Few" had lifted him to a special place. He was near death and couldn't communicate through normal speech, so words meant very little right now. Yet he was taking comfort in the fact that he could look toward his future home in Heaven.

During the concert, his family seated the man in the front row, so we had the opportunity to experience the music through his eyes. As we got close to the time when we would sing "Let My Words Be Few," we could feel the pressure on us grow. We knew how special the song was for this man, and we didn't want to let him down. Emotions usually aren't a friend to performers. It throws off everything—particularly your pitch. Yet this was special.

When we arrived at the intro of "Let My Words Be Few," the man began to thrash violently in his wheelchair. We wondered if he might be dying. His sons were able to discern that though he could no longer use his legs, he wanted to stand during the song. So as he stood to worship, everyone joined together in singing:

> And I'll stand in awe of You, Jesus
> Yes, I'll stand in awe of You
> And I'll let my words be few
> Jesus, I am so in love with You

We don't know how many times we'll sing that song. But there will never be a more memorable time than that night in Minneapolis. After we returned home from that concert tour, we heard from the man's family that he had passed away a few days following that concert.

Today, he is standing, running, and singing in the presence of the Lord. —**Randy, Shawn & Dan**

Lessons from "Let My Words Be Few"

What has God done for you that left you in awe of him?

_____

_____

_____

_____

What does being in love with Jesus look like to you?

_____

_____

_____

_____

_____

If your words are few, how can you show God you love him?

_____

_____

_____

_____

_____

"When your daily life is pleasing to God, then you've accomplished something. This song puts it very simply, let my words be few, and my life speak volumes." —Rick M

"I love this beautiful song so much I kept playing it over and over again. If I had lived in an apartment, the neighbors would've been banging on the floor and walls to cut it out and play something else! Grin." —Zey T

"Jesus is that greatest and deepest love of my life and all it takes is a few words. Thank you." —Karon L

"It's hard to listen to this CD and not have your focus shifted fully to God. Every time I play it, I find myself praising God for all He has done for us." —Mark B

"These guys are truly anointed to bring us into the presence of the Lord." —Leidell G

Our Favorite Bible Verses

When I was nearing the age of thirty, I was wrestling with depression and even contemplated suicide. One of the keys to turning my life around was God's word. I had someone give me a list of Scriptures, and I began to meditate and memorize them. One of the key verses was Deuteronomy 31:8 from the Amplified Bible. It says, "It is the Lord Who goes before you; He will be with you. He will not fail you or abandon you. Do not fear or be dismayed."

Something about that phrase, "He will not . . . abandon you," became a key in my life to remember—that even when you feel like you're alone and forsaken, that God has left you and he doesn't know where you are—in every situation, God will not let you go. That was powerful for me, and I actually wrote a song about it on our first album called, "He'll Never Let You Go." That's really been a key verse for my life and a key point in my life. **—Shawn Craig**

There are a number of Scriptures I've loved through the years. One is Psalm 139:7–10: "Where can I go from Your Spirit? Or where can I flee from Your presence? If I ascend into heaven, You are there; if I make my bed in hell, behold, You are there. If I take the wings of the morning, and dwell in the uttermost parts of the sea, even there Your hand shall lead me, and Your right hand shall hold me" (NKJV).

If we live long enough, I think we all know what it's like to make our bed in Hell and what it's like to feel isolated. And yet the truth of the Scripture is that God's hand will hold you, and his Spirit is there. If you base it on emotion, you may not always feel like he's there, but his word says he's there, and if his word says he's there, then you can believe it, because he never lies. He's right there with you wherever you are, no matter whether you've taken the wings to fly away or you've made your bed in Hell. He's there. David

said that. And that's the word I've stood on for many years.
—**Randy Phillips**

"For by grace you have been saved through faith. And this is not your own doing; it is the gift of God" (Eph. 2:8 ESV). The day I realized that I did not have to work to get God's grace in my life and to be saved was probably one of the greatest awakenings in my life. —**Dan Dean**

New Mercy

Composed by Denise Phillips, Dennis Matkosky,
and Randy Phillips
Album: *Where Strength Begins* (1997)

*"Because of the LORD's great love we are not consumed,
for his compassions never fail. They are new every
morning; great is your faithfulness." (Lam. 3:22–23 NIV)*

I thought that I had crossed the line
Walked away from love one time
Too many
I thought I'd used up all the grace
Set aside for my mistakes
So many

On my knees I found to my surprise
That your mercy renewed with the sunrise

You make Your mercy new every day
You change my life in so many ways
You cradle me in Your sweet grace
You fill me

Yesterday, today, forever more
There's one thing I know for sure
Fresh as the morning dew
You make Your mercy new
Every morning

Oh the wasted times that I have known
A prodigal away from home
Not knowing
Every day Your grace was multiplied
With forgiveness waiting to provide
To save the entire world
How much grace would it take
When the sun comes up
There will be enough

The Story Behind the Song

Anyone who has ever lived in texas knows that there's no
sunrise like a Texas sunrise. No matter where you live, sunrises are beautiful, but in Texas, we do everything bigger
and better (or at least we think we do). That, of course,

holds true for sunrises. One morning as I watched one of these particularly beautiful sunrises, God brought me to Lamentations 3:22–23:

> Because of the Lord's great love
> we are not consumed,
> for his compassions never fail.
> They are new every morning;
> great is your faithfulness. (NIV)

Jeremiah, who wrote those words, had such a thankless job. God had called him to preach to people who didn't want to listen. Throughout his entire ministry, he didn't have a single convert. Yet, out of that brokenness, he wrote these beautiful and inspiring words. I'm sure there were days— many in fact—when Jeremiah thought he was a failure. The prophet desperately needed the mercy of God to rain down on him—and the Lord obliged through a simple sunrise.

I thought about friends, family, and church members who were absolutely convinced they had exhausted the mercy of God, even though he promises us that's impossible. They believed they had sinned too many times, and so they had run out of chances to experience God's mercy.

How often do we buy into this performance-based mentality? We think if we just do a bunch of good things, the Lord will love us more. And if we don't do good works, he'll love us less. But that's just not true. For years now, I've leaned into this truth when I've been tempted to think I have to earn God's love: God can never love me *more* than *he* does right now, whether I'm doing good or bad.

As I reflected on Jeremiah's words in Lamentations, I wrote the words to "New Mercy."

> Every day Your grace was multiplied
> With forgiveness waiting to provide
> To save the entire world
> How much grace would it take
> When the sun comes up
> There will be enough

The words of Lamentations 3:22–23 give us such hope. Every morning, the Lord is granting us new mercy. No matter how far we've gone away from the will of God, no matter how much we've disappointed others, we're never out of chances with our heavenly Father. This should encourage each of us—even in our darkest moments. If the sun comes up, we can be hopeful. If the sun comes up, God can still use us. He has new mercy for us every single morning—no exception.

This truth is not just needed by my friends, family, and church. There are times when I wonder if I have exhausted the mercy of God. Then I take a look at a Texas sunrise.

And God whispers to me—I'm not done with you yet. Thank God for Texas sunrises.—**Randy**

Lessons from "New Mercy"

The song lyrics say, "Yesterday, today, forever more: there's one thing I know for sure. Fresh as the morning dew You make Your mercy new Every morning." How will your life change, knowing that no matter how many mistakes you make or how many times you stumble, God gives you a fresh chance every morning?

_____

_____

_____

_____

_____

_____

_____

Randy says, "This should encourage each of us—even in our darkest moments. If the sun comes up, we can be hopeful. If the sun comes up, God can still use us." Think about a time when you stumbled in sin, yet God still used you for his purposes. Thank God that he pours his grace on you, no matter what you've done.

Randy says, "And God whispers to me—I'm not done with you yet." This means it's never too late to get back on track to complete God's purpose for your life. What do you think about that?

_____

_____

_____

_____

_____

_____

_____

Pastors Who Sing
Phillips, Craig & Dean on Balancing
Music and Church

The three of us are preachers' kids, and we've grown up on the pew. My dad's a second-generation pastor, and my earliest recollection was being in the church. All of us are pastors in our hearts. So when we did our first album with Star Song Records, they said, "Why don't you move to Nashville and serve the Body of Christ globally and get serious about the record business?"

We couldn't do that because we're pastors. We're pastors first, and then we sing as an overflow of that gift. In fact, I incorporate music into my messages. I will sing spontaneously a hymn, a favorite song, or any song that may fit the topic I am preaching on.

I feel like when I'm singing to an audience, they are my congregation. And I love that! I realize that at any particular moment, there are couples in the audience who don't know if they're going to keep their marriage. There are parents there whose children are breaking their heart with their choices. There are people under tremendous economic and emotional stress. I realize that I have about an hour-and-a-half window to allow the Presence of God to pour through me through this music. For those moments, they are my congregation; I am their pastor. I don't see my role at my church or onstage as being any different. **—Randy Phillips**

There's something about going home to my congregation, where there are people who are not necessarily tuned into everything that's happening in Christian music or in the industry or what the charts are doing. Being involved in their lives at a level that doesn't happen when you're onstage helps me to keep everything in perspective. It keeps my feet on the ground. **—Shawn Craig**

I think there's an added dimension of an urgency of the moment, knowing that you're singing and talking to people who at that moment could be going through crises in their lives. There could be a song or something said that night that's going to turn their lives around and cause there to be an awakening of hope that they can go forward. **—Dan Dean**

Singing concerts is really an extension of what we do as pastors. We've always sung, and pastoring was always part of what we were doing. The capacities of being a pastor have changed through the years. Dan and Shawn were music pastors, I was a youth pastor. Through the years, as our senior pastors grew older, we began moving toward the roles of being senior pastors at our churches.

Early in our singing career, we took a lot of dates, sang at every opportunity, every festival, every church service, every radio-promoted event. If they wanted us, we went. And it almost killed us, because we were holding full-time jobs at churches, and we had families to consider. It was what we felt like we needed to do for the first couple of years. Now that we're more established, we're able to plan our schedule more effectively. What is most important to us is our families and our churches. So we prioritize our time so that the tail's not wagging the dog. —**Randy Phillips**

Where Strength Begins

Composed by Connie Harrington, Jim Cooper,
and Shawn Craig
Album: *Where Strength Begins* (1997)

"Not that I have already obtained all this, or have
already been made perfect, but I press on to take hold
of that for which Christ Jesus took hold of me.

"Brothers, I do not consider myself yet to have taken
hold of it. But one thing I do: Forgetting what is behind
and straining toward what is ahead, I press on toward
the goal to win the prize for which God has called me
heavenward in Christ Jesus." (Phil. 3:12–14 NIV)

Here I sit with this cup of life in front of me
I see it's full but I'm afraid to drink
Because I've tried and I've missed the mark
So many times
I can't forget all the hurt inside

But rising up from the ashes
Of these memories
I reach for a hand to save me
And I hear Him Calling

Walk on
Til fear turns to faith and faith becomes sight
Where strength begins
You've got to press on
Move on through the pain
Move on to the place
Where weakness ends
Where strength begins

Here I stand looking to the climb
That's up ahead
I will fall but I'll get up again
Because I know if I keep on walking
Through the fire
I'll be a newer, stronger man of God and I'll

Rise up from the ashes of my memories
And I'll reach for His hand to save me
And I'll hear Him calling

Take up your cross
Get up and walk
Where strength begins

Rising up from the ashes of these memories
I reach for his hand to save me
And I hear Him calling

The Story Behind the Song

I remember seeing a video once about a winter Olympian who would train by going out into the bitter cold where he lived and walking through snowdrifts until he was breathless. After hours of training, he went home and collapsed on the bed.

If you want to get to the level of an Olympian, then the training is tough. You don't match the strength and skill of other world-class athletes without enduring pain. In fact, it's really in the middle of the pain that you find the strength you need to excel.

I thought about that truth—and the video I had seen—one day as I counseled a man at our church. He had been through a few major difficulties—a broken marriage, health issues, etc. As he looked for strength, I told him that we've all been through times when we think we can't go on, when we're at the end of ourselves.

But it's in times like this when God seems to say, "You're right where I want you to be." It's then that we see our next step is in the power of Christ. As we take step by step by step, God begins to do something new in us. But it starts when we admit we're weak. That's where strength begins. Paul tells us this in 2 Corinthians 12:9:

But he said to me, "My grace is
sufficient for you, for my power is
made perfect in weakness."
Therefore I will boast all the more
gladly about my weaknesses, so that
Christ's power may rest on me. (NIV)

One day you get up and you wonder, "How did I get here?" You're feeling stronger. Your energy has returned. You know you didn't get here on your own. You couldn't have. You remember when you were completely washed up, completely out of strength. It's then you realize that you got here by the grace of God. That truth is why I began writing "Where Strength Begins."

Because I know if I keep on walking
Through the fire
I'll be a newer, stronger man of God

I wanted others to discover this amazing truth. Our strength comes when we're at our weakest because that's where God reveals his strength in us. We all need to be reminded of that.
I know I do. **—Shawn**

Lessons from "Where Strength Begins"

The song lyrics say, "Walk on until fear turns to faith and faith becomes sight . . ." When have you had a "Where Strength Begins" situation, where God guided you from fear to faith to sight?

_____

_____

_____

_____

_____

_____

Shawn says, "You remember when you were completely washed up, completely out of strength. It's then you realize that you got here by the grace of God." When have you been strengthened by nothing but the grace of God?

_____

_____

_____

_____

_____

How have you seen God's power work through your weakness (See 2 Corinthians 12:9 below)?

_____

_____

_____

_____

_____

_____

"'My grace is sufficient for you, for my power is made perfect in weakness.' Therefore I will boast all the more gladly about my weaknesses, so that Christ's power may rest on me" (2 Cor. 12:9 NIV).

_____

_____

_____

_____

_____

_____

_____

A Dream Will Cost You
By Shawn Craig

When I was a kid, we would often head to Grandma's house for Thanksgiving. It was eight hundred miles away, so sometimes we would leave at night. It was fun to be carried to the car half asleep and wake up the next morning almost halfway there. I closed my eyes at home and opened them over four hundred miles away. Cool.

Some people think about their futures like that:

- I can't wait for my dream job. It's gonna be fun when I can afford the flat screen, the new car, the boat . .
- I'm praying and hoping for my future. I know God has big plans for me. I know it's on the way!
- Someday, I'll have a wonderful family with a spouse that loves me. I can't wait.
- I have my phone on because I'm expecting that call that will change my life!

As people get older, sometimes disillusionment sets in. People get discouraged and sometimes give up. We soon begin to realize that a destiny is not a destination. Dreams don't just come true without effort. Diligence is required. Dreams cost something.

- Your dream job may mean going back to school. That will cost you money, time, and sleep.

- God's big plans for you may cost you some years in obscurity like Moses, David, and Paul.
- Your "dreamy" family will cost diligent effort to maintain healthy and loving relationships. Otherwise, your dream may become a nightmare!

Dreams will cost us. The bigger the dream, often the higher the price will be. But it's the journey that God wants us to enjoy. Don't just close your eyes and hope for the best. Keep your eyes wide open all along the way. Every mile there's something to learn about Jesus and his friendship with us. And whatever the cost is, as long as you're walking with Jesus, it's worth it all!

Blessing in the Thorn

**Composed by David Allen Clark, Don Koch,
and Randy Phillips**
Album: *Where Strength Begins* (1997)

"*Therefore, so that I would not exalt myself, a thorn
in the flesh was given to me, a messenger of Satan to
torment me so I would not exalt myself.*

"*Concerning this, I pleaded with the Lord three
times to take it away from me. But He said to me, 'My
grace is sufficient for you, for power is perfected in
weakness.' Therefore, I will most gladly boast all the
more about my weaknesses, so that Christ's power
may reside in me.*

"*So I take pleasure in weaknesses, insults,
catastrophes, persecutions, and in pressures, because
of Christ. For when I am weak, then I am strong.*"
(2 Cor. 12:7–10 HCSB)

I read about a man of God who gloried in his weakness
And I wish that I could be more like Him and less like me
Am I to blame for what I'm not or is pain the way God

teaches me to grow
I need to know

When does the thorn become a blessing?
When does the pain become a friend?
When does the weakness make me stronger?
When does my faith make me whole again?
I want to feel His arms around me
In the middle of my raging storm
So that I can see the blessing in the thorn

I've heard it said the strength of Christ is perfect in my
weakness
And the more that I go through, the more I prove the
promise true
His love will go to any length and reaches even now to
where I am
But tell me once again

When does the thorn become a blessing?
When does the pain become a friend?
When does the weakness make me stronger?
When does my faith make me whole again?
I want to feel His arms around me
In the middle of my raging storm
So that I can see the blessing in the thorn

Lord, I have to ask You
On the cross You suffered through

Was there a time You ever doubted
What You already knew?

When does the thorn become a blessing?
When does the pain become a friend?
When does the weakness make me stronger?
When does my faith make me whole again?
I want to feel His arms around me
In the middle of my raging storm
So that I can see the blessing in the thorn

I want to feel the blessing in the thorn

The Story Behind the Song

Garwin Dobyns Always Called Himself a "one-in-a-million." It wasn't some arrogant statement designed to bring attention to his uniqueness. He had a disease that only one in a million people truly have—progressive myositis ossificans. It's a disease where the soft tissues in the body calcify and basically turn into bone. It's incredibly painful and debilitating. My friend, who was a member of the church where I pastored, had lived with it most of his life.

The disease was so rare that surgeons would fly in from all over the country to examine Garwin, because progressive myositis ossificans is something they'd read about in textbooks, but they'd likely never encounter in their lifetimes. Garwin called the disease his "babe ministry" because through it he got to meet so many beautiful women—including the Dallas Cowboys cheerleaders.

Despite the painful and difficult disease, this man was the most cheerful, friendly guy I have ever met. He never missed church. Instead, he'd show up early. Always encouraging, he'd leave voice messages on my phone letting me know how much he enjoyed my sermons. He had been able to take this terribly difficult disease and make it into something beautiful.

I asked Garwin one day, "How do you do it? You don't seem to be angry with God. I don't sense any faith crisis with you."

He then began to describe how grateful he was to have life. He told me that every time these top physicians from around the world would fly in to see him, he had the opportunity to testify to the glory of Jesus—and all that the Lord had done for him.

Paul described a "thorn in the flesh" in 2 Corinthians 12—one that brought glory to God as he worked through the apostle's weakness. In a similar way, Garwin's illness brought glory and honor to God.

Paul asked God to remove his thorn three times, but God wouldn't do it. Instead, the Lord told Paul, "My grace is sufficient." The challenge for Paul—and for Garwin—is to find the blessing in the thorn.

With the help of Don Koch, I wrote this song for all the Garwins out there. For everyone out there who has been given such a difficult, debilitating challenge. I wanted them to know that despite the obvious pains they have, there's a blessing in the thorn.—**Randy**

Lessons from "Blessing in the Thorn"

The song lyrics say, "Is pain the way God teaches me to grow?" What do you think about that? When was a time that difficult circumstances or a painful event deepened your faith in God? Explain what happened?

_____

_____

_____

_____

_____

_____

_____

_____

The song lyrics ask, "When does the thorn become a blessing? When does the pain become a friend? When does the weakness make me stronger? When does my faith make me whole again?" How has God turned a thorn in your life into a true blessing?

_____

_____

_____

_____

_____

_____

_____

God says he will work through your weaknesses; how does
that change the way you see them?

_____

_____

_____

_____

_____

_____

_____

_____

_____

_____

_____

Blessings from Our Thorns

God uses pain to shape us into people who are more like Jesus and more able to minister to the very real needs of the people around us. Randy Phillips, Shawn Craig, and Dan Dean are no different. Here are some significant situations where God shaped their ministry through painful experiences—and how they've been able to use that pain to minister to others.

The Hard Work of Marriage

On New Years Eve 2002, my wife Becky and I were involved in a violent collision. I was going about fifty-five miles-per-hour when a pickup truck pulled right in front of me off a side road. The miracle really started the night before.

My father-in-law had a dream that my wife and I were in a car accident. In the dream, I was killed and my wife was seriously injured. He woke up so disturbed that he got out of bed, prayed, and interceded for us. We believe those prayers spared our lives.

The second miracle occurred when a lady happened to be ten feet from our car and got to my wife and kept her still. My wife had already opened the door and was trying to get out. That would have been disastrous. We later discovered that she suffered the same fracture Christopher Reeves suffered—she had broken C2 in her neck and her back at L1. We were told that if she had moved, she easily could have died.

So 2003 was a rough year. She spent four months immobile in a hospital bed and then in physical therapy. It was quite an ordeal. But I'm happy to say she fully recovered—no paralysis. It's an amazing miracle. We're so blessed.

Long-term, the accident brought us much closer together. On a short-term basis, it was an adventure that neither one of us had ever walked through. I have to admit, there were days when I was emotionally disconnected—I didn't want to be, but I think it was a matter of survival. I had to shake myself several times and say, "You can't do this," and I'd pull myself back. It was a long, hard thing to walk through.

My wife is a totally different person today. Both of us have learned how to appreciate life more and learn that some things don't matter in the grand scheme of things. We've made a commitment to each other and to our children that those things that are secondary—what we have no control over—we're not going to worry about.

I don't talk about this very often, but before PC&D got together, at about year ten of our marriage, we hit the wall. If you had talked to me at that time, I would have said there is no way we'll survive. It was a very dire situation. I thought I would be forced out of ministry, there was no hope, and our marriage was collapsing.

We were married very young. We just thought it was a cool thing to do. Our parents encouraged us to be married. We never even knew if we were compatible.

Back then, I shared our hardship with my pastor, and his advice was "don't tell anyone." So we didn't. For ten years, we struggled and stumbled. But in year ten God led us to a wonderful Christian counselor, and she totally turned our lives around. She put tools in our hands, helped us to work on our marriage, and simply listened to us. We moved from a hopeless marriage into a loving, hopeful, God-centered marriage relationship.

I'm saying this to encourage people to get help. Don't go it alone. Especially men. Men often turn their backs on problems. They tend not to discuss these things or seek accountability. There are some wonderful people and great tools out there.

God saved our marriage. It took a lot of counseling, prayer, and hard work. I saw God use something that was so piercingly painful that it was hard to talk about. Through that thorn in my marriage, I've been able to help many other people with their marriages.

And that's who we are. We're simply sick people who get healing and help other people. **—Dan Dean**

Dark Days of Depression

If you've never experienced darkness, trying to describe it to someone else is like trying to describe chocolate to someone who has never tasted it. It just doesn't make sense. Before I went through my own period of depression, it never made any sense to me. When I would hear about people in depression or despair, I wondered why people couldn't just "cheer up" and "get through it."

But when I went through a period of darkness in my life, I realized I had no idea what I was talking about before. You can't cheer yourself up from despair. You feel powerless. It's this big blanket that is thrown over you. You feel like you're going to suffocate. I've always loved the sun and daytime, but during that period I learned to dread the daytime.

You can do certain things to help during those periods, but you can't just wish it away. It's impossible.

My period of darkness also helped me see how much I needed the Lord. It's like breathing. You never know how much you need air until you've been without it. Now I'm so much more grateful for the day-by-day blessings. I'm much more dependent upon God.

I wouldn't want to go through it again, but I'm grateful for how God used this period to make me more compassionate and more aware of how much I needed him.
—**Shawn Craig**

Blessing in the Thorn: *Testimonies*

"There is a little book called *Hinds' Feet on High Places*; it was written in 1948 as an allegory to a Christian's life journey. The main character, a young woman, decides to follow the

'Shepherd' to the high places where He promises her, her life will be transformed and she can find victory in every circumstance. At the beginning of the journey he places a thorn in her heart. At the end of the book he removes it and with it He tears all the things out that have grown up around it.

"After reading the book at least twice I still had trouble fully understanding the purpose of the thorn. The first time I listened to 'Blessing In The Thorn' I finally made a connection. If I hadn't read the book, I wouldn't have understood the meaning of the song exactly, but the two together brought understanding.

"Life is hard and understanding circumstances is a big enough challenge much less accepting them; but that's the entire secret to living in peace. The song, like many others, is an expression of feelings I didn't know how to express."
—Carla

"'Blessing in the Thorn' is a particular comfort to me because it shows no matter what 'thorns' we experience, God will always be there." —Courtney H

"These gifted artists have graced my Christian walk with their songs. 'The Blessing in the Thorn' speaks clearly to anyone who has ever experienced life's deepest pain. I believe God uses music to minister to our soul. He is using these men in a mighty way." —Avid

"Shed tears over 'Blessing in the Thorn.' Friends sent us this CD when my wife was in chemotherapy treatment for breast cancer. They said, 'Listen to "Blessing in the Thorn."' We put it in the CD player, sat in our living room, and cried. The words and music tenderly reached right in to where we were. It definitely touched a chord. It reminded us of the truth of Scripture: 'for when I am weak, then I am strong, for His strength is made perfect in our weakness.'" —Bill B

"'Blessing in the Thorn' helps us be like Paul and 'glory in his weakness' and bring you to tears wanting to 'feel His arms around me in the middle of the raging storm, so that I can see the blessing in the thorn.'" —TB

Just One

Composed by Connie Harrington and Jim Cooper
Album: *Where Strength Begins* (1997)

*"I am the way and the truth and the life. No one comes
to the Father except through me." (John 14:6 NIV)*

Ask what changes a man
And the answers are a dime a dozen
Points of view are like sand
Stretching out as far as the eye can see
There's a thousand different philosophies

But there's just one book
And there's just one name
With the power to heal and the grace to save
You can search the world for another way
But if you're lookin' for the road to be on
There's just one

There's too much at stake
To be wasting time on imitations
Promises and claims

There will never be a substitute
For the blood, the word, and the simple truth

'Cause there's just one book
And there's just one name
With the power to heal and the grace to save
You can search the world for another way
But if you're lookin' for the road to be on
There's just one

Door to open where truth and hope will be
Waiting there on the other side
Just one story that's never-ending
With life beginning in Jesus Christ

You can search the world for another way
But if you're lookin' for the road to be on
There's just one

The Story Behind the Song

When Connie Harrington—who later became one of
America's best country music writers—penned this song,

religious pluralism was gaining in popularity. Oprah was telling the world that every religion could lead to God—and people were buying it.

Today, nearly twenty years later, those days seem almost quaint. We live in a world where everyone seems convinced you can get to God through all sorts of avenues—except Jesus. You hear it all the time—if you're good enough, religious enough, nice enough, then you can make your way to God. Pick a religion—any religion. It doesn't really matter.

As pastors, this has become a critical issue to us. Families can't escape it. Years ago there weren't as many points of view and perceptions being directed at those we shepherd as there are today. A generation or two ago, you had to worry when kids went off to college that they'd be exposed to different worldviews for the first time. Today that concern starts much earlier.

Even as toddlers, our children are taught that it doesn't really matter who you believe in or who you pray to; it only matters that you're sincere.

Yet the Bible presents a starkly different view. Jesus says, "I am the way and the truth and the life. No one comes to the Father except through me" (John 14:6NIV).

Jesus gives no other option for our access to God. "I am the way," he says. That may be old-fashioned. That may seem out of date. That may seem rude and exclusionary to others. We get that. It's hard to think about our friends and family who don't have a relationship with God through Jesus and realize what that means for their eternal destiny.

Yet it's Jesus's own words. This isn't based on our own opinions. The One who tossed the stars into the sky and carved out the oceans told us this. We have no reason to doubt it.

That's the truth we wanted to communicate through this song—there's just one way to God.

That one way is Jesus. Why is that important? The song lyrics make the case.

> There's too much at stake
> To be wasting time on imitations
> Promises and claims
> There will never be a substitute
> For the blood, the word, and the simple truth

We've staked our whole lives and ministries upon the basic message of this song.—**Randy, Craig & Dan**

Lessons from "Just One"

The song lyrics say, "But there's just one book, And there's just one name With the power to heal and the grace to save." How does this relate to this verse: "Salvation is to be found through him alone; in all the world there is no one else whom God has given who can save us" (Acts 4:12 TEV)?

_____

_____

_____

_____

_____

Randy, Shawn & Dan say, "Even as toddlers, our children are taught that it doesn't really matter who you believe in or who you pray to; it only matters that you're sincere. Yet the Bible presents a starkly different view. Jesus says, 'I am the way and the truth and the life. No one comes to the Father except through me' (John 14:6 NIV)." How can you respond to people in a loving manner when they say there are many roads to heaven?

_____

_____

_____

_____

_____

Mediate on this passage:

> Now God has us where he wants us, with all the
> time in this world and the next to shower grace
> and kindness upon us in Christ Jesus. Saving is
> all his idea, and all his work. All we do is trust
> him enough to let him do it. It's God's gift from
> start to finish!
>
> We don't play the major role. If we did, we'd
> probably go around bragging that we'd done the
> whole thing! No, we neither make nor save our-
> selves. God does both the making and saving. He
> creates each of us by Christ Jesus to join him in
> the work he does, the good work he has gotten
> ready for us to do, work we had better be doing.
>
> But don't take any of this for granted. It was
> only yesterday that you outsiders to God's ways
> had no idea of any of this, didn't know the first
> thing about the way God works, hadn't the faint-
> est idea of Christ. You knew nothing of that rich

25 for 25

history of God's covenants and promises in Israel, hadn't a clue about what God was doing in the world at large.

Now because of Christ—dying that death, shedding that blood—you who were once out of it altogether are in on everything. (Eph. 2:7–13 *The Message*)

What is God telling you about this passage? How might it apply to your life?

_____

_____

_____

_____

_____

_____

_____

"For God loved the world so much that he gave his one and only Son, so that everyone who believes in him will not perish but have eternal life. God sent his Son into the world not to judge the world, but to save the world through him" (John 3:16–17 NLT).

Mercy Came Running

Composed by Dan Dean, David Allen Clark, and Don Koch
Album: *Trust* (1995)

"The Word became flesh and made his dwelling among us. We have seen his glory, the glory of the One and Only, who came from the Father, full of grace and truth." (John 1:14 NIV)

Once there was a holy place
Evidence of God's embrace
And I can almost see Mercy's face
Pressed against the veil

Looking down with longing eyes
Mercy must have realized
That once His blood was sacrificed
Freedom would prevail

And as the sky grew dark
And the earth began to shake
With justice no longer in the way

Mercy came running
Like a prisoner set free
Past all my failures
To the point of my need
When the sin that I carried
Was all I could see
And when I could not reach mercy
Mercy came running to me

Once there was a broken heart
Way too human from the start
And all the years left you torn apart
Hopeless and afraid

Walls I never meant to build
Left this prisoner unfulfilled
Freedom called but even still
It seemed so far away

I was bound by the chains
From the wages of my sin
Just when I felt like giving in

Mercy came running
Like a prisoner set free
Past all my failures
To the point of my need
When the sin that I carried
Was all I could see

And when I could not reach mercy
Mercy came running to me

Sometimes I still feel so far
So far from where I really should be
He gently calls to my heart
Just to remind me

Mercy came running
Like a prisoner set free
Past all my failures
To the point of my need
When the sin that I carried
Was all I could see
And when I could not reach mercy
Mercy came running

Mercy came running
Like a prisoner set free
Past all my failures
To the point of my need
When the sin that I carried
Was all I could see
And when I could not reach mercy
Mercy came running

Mercy came running
Like a prisoner set free
Past all my failures

To the point of my need
When the sin that I carried
Was all I could see
And when I could not reach mercy
Mercy came running

The Story Behind the Song

Years ago I heard a great sermon that has never quite left me. Preaching through Psalm 85:10, "Mercy and truth are met together; righteousness and peace have kissed each other" (KJV), the pastor gave a memorable illustration. In the Old Testament, he told us, mercy was trapped in the Most Holy Place.

Consider the story of Achan in Joshua 7. His entire family was stoned because the Law required it in response to his sin. When the Law made a pronouncement, there was no room for consideration, no place for mercy.

As the pastor preached about Achan and what the Law required, he described a particularly unforgettable scene.

Mercy sits in the Most Holy Place with its face pressed up against the veil looking out over Israel and saying, "If I could get out of here, I could stop this from happening."

That picture of mercy, ready and willing to come out if freed, stays with me. Jesus tore down the veil, and God's mercy—which had once been limited to the Most Holy Place—now roams the earth freely.

I love that vision of mercy running to meet a waiting world. That's a great picture of the mercy of Jesus. In the song, Dave Clark, Don Koch, and I described the scene like this:

> Mercy came running
> Like a prisoner set free
> Past all my failures
> To the point of my need
> When the sin that I carried
> Was all I could see
> And when I could not reach mercy
> Mercy came running to me

The Bible reminds us of this awesome combination of truth and grace that came in Jesus. "The Word became flesh and made his dwelling among us. We have seen his glory, the glory of the one and only Son, who came from the Father, full of grace and truth" (John 1:14 NIV). The great mystery and wonder we have in Christ is that it includes both justice and mercy, righteousness and peace.

When Jesus was crucified, everything radically changed. As the thick veil to the Most Holy Place was torn away, God signaled to all who would hear that Christ's broken body provides the way to God's mercy.

I am forever thankful for that.

This was the first time in my life that I co-wrote a song with a Nashville writer. I've discovered through the years that there is strength in numbers when it comes to song-writing. Dave, Don, and I put this together in about an hour and a half. When I walked out of the building that day, I knew we had written something pretty special. **—Dan**

Lessons from "Mercy Came Running"

How have you seen God's Mercy come running to you?

_____

_____

_____

_____

_____

_____

_____

_____

The Bible says, "The Word became flesh . . . full of grace and truth" (John 1:14 NIV). Why is that combination of grace and truth so important to our relationship with Jesus?

_____

_____

_____

_____

_____

_____

_____

_____

_____

The Bible says, "Surely His salvation is near to those who fear Him, That glory may dwell in our land. Mercy and truth have met together; Righteousness and peace have kissed. Truth shall spring out of the earth, And righteousness shall look down from heaven" (Ps. 85:9–11 NKJV). What does this tell you about God's efforts to reach you no matter how far you've run from him?

_____

_____

_____

_____

_____

_____

_____

_____

Testimonies about PC&D's Music

"Phillips, Craig & Dean's music is such a blessing on my drive to work in the morning. Yes, I do lift a hand in priase (keep the other on the wheel!) as the music lifts me to give glory to the Lord of Lords and the King of Kings!" —Bonnie S

"Their music is created by individuals who know the Lord personally and who desire to spread his love through the means of their talent. Your spirit can't help but worship as you listen or sing along with the songs." —Anonymous

"If this music doesn't light your fire, your wood's wet. I'm a typical guy with typical guy emotions. I usually listen more to the production and arrangement of a song than I do the words. There are . . . songs that force me to pay attention to the words and bring me to my knees, sobbing and humbling God almost every time I hear them.

"If you want to take a few minutes to soak in God's grace after dealing with a tough day or tough situation, then listen to Phillips, Craig & Dean's music. If you listen with your heart, the praise will be inevitable." —KS

"I cannot thank the three of you enough for sharing your gifts and talent and allowing God to use you. I am so thankful that I can praise God and worship him even when I have experienced loss. Singing praise to God in my head has given me emotional strength when I have needed it." —Tania

"This group has the anointing of God on their lives and they always bless us with their music." —Michele

"I use the song from this album 'I Want to Be Just Like You' in my Redirecting Children's Behavior parenting course . . . parents love it . . . it really touches us, as parents, where *we live.* The music is so inspiring and so beautiful . . . I feel so peaceful when I listen to this music. Phillips, Craig & Dean are the best Christian artists recording today in *my* opinion. You can *feel the holy spirit* alive in their music and in the lyrics . . . this music *moves* you in a very positive, uplifting, spiritual way." —Anonymous

"'New Mercy' reminded me that whatever I may do, God's grace covers me even then." —PianoPlayer

"There is *nothing* like telling it like it really is!!! I have loved P, C & D as long as i have known of them. Their songs helped when the unimaginably horrible happened to some precious young people who went to school with our children.

"'Pour My Love on You,' 'This Is How It Feels to Be Free,' 'Favorite Song of All,' 'When God Ran' . . . just so many *great* songs with such a profound anointing!!!" —HeHumbled

"'Mercy Came Running like a Prisoner Set Free.' I love this song. I listen to it daily. God wants to give us his mercy. We just have to reach out for it." —KHjart

I've Got You Covered

Composed by Dan Dean, David Allen Clark, and Don Koch
Album: *Restoration* (1999)

*"This righteousness from God comes through faith in
Jesus Christ to all who believe. There is no difference, for
all have sinned and fall short of the glory of God, and
are justified freely by his grace through the redemption
that came by Christ Jesus." (Rom. 3:22–24 NIV)*

A scene so familiar at the old five and dime
The little boy waited his turn in line
And with eyes so intent he proudly displayed
The candy he'd buy with the money he'd saved

The girl at the counter wasn't sure what to do
'Cause the money was less than the price that was due
Then a stranger spoke up from his place in line
Said whatever he's short just take it and add it to mine

I've got you covered, I'll pay the difference
You don't have to worry at all
Whatever the cost is I'll go the distance

If you fail, I will catch you
You know I won't let you feel like you're there all alone
I've got you covered

Sometimes when I look back it's hard to explain
Just how far I've come yet how little has changed
I still long to hold what seems so out of reach
Only to find out it's not what it seems

I come to the Father alone and afraid
In need of forgiveness yet it's so far away
I cry out for mercy a child so in need
With a voice of compassion the Father calls out to me

I know what you're facing, I see where you're standing
I'm holding all the answers you need
'Cause no situation will ever take you out of My reach

The Story Behind the Song

My father-in-law, who was a pastor, once illustrated the
grace of God by using the talented Olympian Carl Lewis,

who received the gold medal in the long jump in four Olympics in a row. My father-in-law is no Olympian by any stretch of the imagination. Yet he realized that if he and Carl Lewis were to try to jump from one side of the Grand Canyon to the other, the result would be the same. Neither would stand a chance.

We all have the same chance in having a relationship with God based upon our own effort. The Bible teaches us, "All have sinned and fall short of the glory of God," (Rom. 3:23), and "The wages of sin is death" (Rom. 6:23).

Those twin truths would be pretty depressing if they weren't offset by the grace of God. We'll never be good enough to gain access to God; we can only do so by the gift of God's grace. The grace we need from God is far beyond anything that we could furnish on our own.

As my father-in-law preached about our need for grace those many years ago, he shared the illustration that became the first verse of "I've Got You Covered."

We've all probably been in a similar situation. A kid tries to buy something at the grocery store but doesn't quite have the money. Someone else in line pays the price he can't pay.

That's what Jesus did for us. He paid the price we couldn't pay. He covered it all. **—Dan**

Lessons from "I've Got You Covered"

The song lyrics say, "Whatever the cost is, I'll go the distance." What does this say about God's ability to forgive? Can you ever run past the reach of God's grace? Why or why not?

_____

_____

_____

_____

_____

_____

_____

The song lyrics say, "If you fail, I will catch you." Is there a dream God has given you that you are not pursuing because you're afraid to fail? What if you trusted God to catch you if you fail? How would that change things?

_____

_____

_____

_____

_____

_____

_____

_____

Dan says, "We'll never be good enough to gain access to God; we can only do so by the gift of God's grace. The grace we need from God is far beyond anything that we could furnish on our own." What does this statement mean to you? How is it related to your walk with Jesus?

_____

_____

_____

_____

_____

_____

_____

"For the wages of sin is death, but the gift of God is eternal life in Christ Jesus our Lord" (Rom. 6:23 NIV).

This Is How It Feels to Be Free

Composed by David Allen Clark, Don Koch,
and Shawn Craig
Album: *Where Strength Begins* (1997)

*"So if the Son sets you free, you will be free indeed . . .
Now the Lord is the Spirit, and where the Spirit of the
Lord is, there is freedom" (John 8:36; 2 Cor. 3:17 NIV).*

There is a wall that has been standing
Since the day that Adam fell
Sin is where it started
And Sin is why it held
Speakin' as a prisoner
Who was there and lived to tell
I remember how it felt

I could hear the sound of freedom
Like a distant voice it called
And beckoned me to follow
Where I had never gone
And though my heart was willin'

I just stood there at the wall
Prayin' somehow it would fall

But in a cross I found a doorway
And a hand that held a key
And when the chains fell at my feet
For the first time I could see

Chorus:
This is how it feels to be free
This is what it means to know that
I am forgiven
This is how it feels to be free
To see that life can be more than I imagined
This is how it feels to be free
This is how it feels to be free

There are days when I'm reminded
Of the prison I was in
Like a livin' nightmare
Burning from within
I can feel the voice of evil
I can hear the call of sin
But I won't go back again

See, once I tasted freedom
Then the walls could bind no more
Since mercy gave me wings to fly
Like an eagle I can soar

25 for 25

Chorus:

Somewhere there's a prison
Where the chains still bind
and there but for the grace of God
Those walls could still be mine
So for all the captives I say

Chorus

The Story Behind the Song

You've probably seen the pictures. It's happened dozens of times over the past few decades. After years of repression, a country is liberated, and its people are set free. You'll see photos of people celebrating their newly found freedom. Those photos are often infectious—in part because the feeling of freedom is infectious.

You can see smiles that are big and eyes that are alive.

These photos are a quick glimpse into how it feels to be free. The feeling of political freedom is enormously powerful, but it is nothing like the feeling of spiritual freedom.

It's possible there's no more significant doctrine in Scripture than the one that details the freedom available to all those who believe in a crucified and resurrected Savior. The Bible provides so much rich teaching on the topic—from Jesus himself in John 8:36 to Paul in 2 Corinthians 3:17 and Galatians 5:13–14.

The doctrine of our freedom in Christ is foundational to our faith.

But as important as it is to immerse ourselves in what Scripture teaches about our freedom in Christ, we can never forget what it feels like to be free. It's life-changing to truly understand that you're free from your old life—free to be the person he created you to be.

I took this idea to Dave Clark and Don Koch. I told them I wanted to write a song—not about the doctrine of freedom in Christ—but about the feeling of freedom. After I explained the idea, Dave started typing away. In a few minutes, he asked, "What do you think about this?"

> There is a wall that has been standing
> Since the day that Adam fell
> Sin is where it started
> And Sin is why it held
> Speakin' as a prisoner
> Who was there and lived to tell
> I remember how it felt

He nailed it. Those first few lines by Dave really inspired us. We started feeding off each other's ideas, working together to hammer out the rest of the lyrics. It doesn't happen like that all the time, but it did on this song. Everything came together smoothly and quickly.

We've had the opportunity to sing this song several times with the Brooklyn Tabernacle Choir. We'd look back on stage and see a choir filled with people of different ages, nationalities, races, and backgrounds. Even though our lives were totally different, all of us could boldly sing—This is how it feels to be free. This is what it means to know that I am forgiven.

That has to be what Heaven is like. —**Shawn**

Lessons from "This Is How It Feels to Be Free"

What does living a life free in Christ look like?

_____

_____

_____

_____

_____

_____

If you fully understood how much God loves and forgives you, it would transform your life. Why do you think this is true?

_____

_____

_____

_____

_____

According to Galatians 5:13–14 (see below), what is an act of true freedom?

_____

_____

_____

_____

_____

_____

Galatians 5:13–14—It is absolutely clear that God has called you to a free life. Just make sure that you don't use this freedom as an excuse to do whatever you want to do and destroy your freedom. Rather, use your freedom to serve one another in love; that's how freedom grows.

For everything we know about God's Word is summed up in a single sentence: Love others as you love yourself. That's an act of true freedom. (*The Message*)

Crucified with Christ

Composed by David Allen Clark, Denise Phillips,
Don Koch, and Randy Phillips
Album: *Trust* (1995)

*"I have been crucified with Christ and I no longer live,
but Christ lives in me. The life I live in the body, I live
by faith in the Son of God, who loved me and gave
himself for me.*

*"I do not set aside the grace of God, for if righteous-
ness could be gained through the law, Christ died for
nothing!" (Gal. 2:20–21 NIV).*

As I look back
On what I thought was living
I'm amazed at the price
I chose to pay
And to think I ignored
What really mattered
'Cause I thought the sacrifice
Would be too great

But when I finally reached
The point of giving in
I found the cross
Was calling even then
And even though
It took dying to survive
I've never felt so much alive

For I am crucified with Christ
And yet I live
Not I but Christ
That lives within me

His Cross will never ask for more
Than I can give
For it's not my strength but His
There's no greater sacrifice
For I am crucified with Christ
And yet I live

As I hear the Savior
Call for daily dying
I will bow beneath
The weight of Calvary
Let my hands surrender
To His piercing purpose
That holds me to the cross
Yet sets me free

I will glory in
The power of the cross
The things I thought were gain
I count as loss
And with His suffering
I identify
And by His resurrection power
I am alive

For I am crucified with Christ
And yet I live
Not I but Christ
That lives within me

His Cross will never ask for more
Than I can give
For it's not my strength but His
There's no greater sacrifice
For I am crucified with Christ
And yet I live

And I will offer all I have
So that His cross is not in vain
For I found to live is Christ
And to die is truly gain

For I am crucified with Christ
And yet I live

25 for 25

Not I but Christ
That lives within me

His Cross will never ask for more
Than I can give
For it's not my strength but His
There's no greater sacrifice
For I am crucified with Christ
And yet I live

For I am crucified with Christ
And yet I live

"Crucified with Christ"
GMA Dove Nomination—Inspirational Song of the Year, 1997
GMA Dove Nomination—Song of Year, 1997
Inspirational Song of the Decade—1990s (*CCM Magazine*, 2000)

The Story Behind the Song

I was going through a particularly tough time when God
began to impress this song upon my heart. I remember
feeling a great weight pressing against me. As I studied

Scripture, the Lord took me to Galatians 2:20–21, the passage quoted right above this song.

As I read Paul's words about being "crucified with Christ," I knew I had to get to that point where I could lay down my agenda and pick up the Lord's. I needed to get to the cross. It was clearly decision time for me.

As I pondered what God was doing in my life, I started thinking about the words to this song. That's when I called Don Koch and Dave Clark, and we began to craft the song together. God clearly touched the writing process because the words flowed quickly.

My hope has always been that this song is an encouragement for all who ask themselves, "Is there a cost to the Christian life?" Of course there is! "Do we have struggles and pain as we follow Jesus?" No doubt. The Bible never flinches from answering those two questions. I believe this song communicates that truth.

What doesn't challenge us won't change us.

Galatians 2 is a clarion call for us to humble ourselves, take up our cross, and follow Jesus. And I think the message that we must be crucified with Christ is why this song has meant so much to so many people over the past two decades.

The cross and the resurrection mean everything to us as a group. They are cornerstones to our ministry and have been so for the past twenty-five years.

That's what this song is all about—the cross. When the song came out, it was Number Two in the country for a long time. Despite how much the song seemed to connect with people, one radio station refused to play it. The station happened to be one of the largest at that time. When someone asked the station's programmer why he wasn't playing it, he answered, "I just don't know whether the cross resonates with our listeners."

I've since been involved in that programmer's life because of a variety of seismic events he has gone through. As we've talked about those painful issues, his entire attitude has changed. Over and over again, I've heard him say, "I don't know how this is going to turn out, but if I can just get back to the cross, I think I'll be alright."

Amen. —**Randy**

Lessons from "Crucified with Christ"

What does it mean to be "crucified with Christ"? How should this change the way you live?

_____

_____

_____

_____

_____

_____

_____

_____

Randy says, "My hope has always been that this song is an encouragement for all of those who ask themselves, 'Is there a cost to the Christian life?' Of course there is!" Talk about the cost of allowing Christ to live through you. What has it cost you personally?

_____

_____

Randy says, "What doesn't challenge us won't change us." What do you think about this statement?

Crucified with Christ: *Testimonies*

"My favorite song by Phillips, Craig & Dean is 'Crucified With Christ.' I listen to that song all the time when I'm struggling with life. Your music keeps me together. Your music is a blessing to me." —Renee Dawn Faith Benise

"I love this song. The Apostle Paul said, 'I die daily. We put off the old self and live for Christ.'" —KH

"Such a tremendous song that ministers to your soul!! It really inspires you, as well as reminds you of what is important." —PP

"Only the Bible offers us the word of God, but PC&D have put verses and biblical thoughts into a wonderful blend of contemporary music." —Anonymous

Shine On Us

Composed by Deborah Smith and Michael W. Smith
Album: *My Utmost for His Highest* (1995)

"Let the light of your face shine upon us, O LORD"
(Ps. 4:6 NIV).

Lord, let Your light
Light of Your face
Shine on us

Lord, let Your light
Light of Your face
Shine on us

That we may be saved
That we may have life
To find our way
In the darkest night
Let your light shine on us

Lord, let Your grace
Grace from Your hand
Come over us

Lord, let Your grace
Grace from Your hand
Come over us

That we may be saved
That we may have life
To find our way
In the darkest night
Let Your grace come over us

Lord, let Your love
Love with no end
Come over us

Lord, let Your love
Love with no end
Come over us

That we may be saved
That we may have life
To find our way
In the darkest night
Let Your love come over us
Let Your light shine on us

"Shine On Us" appears on the album *My Utmost for His Highest* Dove
Award for Special Event Album of the Year (1995) Nominated for Grammy
Award Best Pop / Contemporary Gospel Album (1995)

The Story Behind the Song

We never expected anyone to ask us to be a part of an album like *My Utmost for His Highest*. It was such an honor to add our voices to a compilation that showed appreciation for the great Oswald Chambers and his unforgettable devotional.

Then, when we saw the list of artists who would be a part of this album—people such as Michael W. Smith, Amy Grant, and Steven Curtis Chapman—we couldn't help but wonder what we were doing on the list. We kind of wondered whether it was a mistake. Yet we recognized it was a tremendous privilege, so we crossed our fingers and jumped on in.

In the years since "Shine On Us" debuted, we've heard over and over from people who have used it at a wedding or a funeral or a graduation. Often, as followers of Jesus, we invoke the image of light as we're taking a step into the unknown. New stages frighten us. We reach out in those days for the light of Jesus. That's what this song is all about.

As the words of the song go, in those days we look to God: "To find our way in the darkest night."

The truth is, it doesn't matter how dark the day, how deep the valley, how painful the depression, the light of Jesus is available to all of us. We know the One who brings light to dark. The psalmist says of the Lord:

> Even the darkness will not be dark to you;
> the night will shine like the day,
> for darkness is as light to you. (Ps. 139:12NIV)

One of the top moments in the past twenty-five years of our ministry has been when we had the opportunity to perform this song at the famous Ryman Auditorium in Nashville. Though we had been to the theater before, we'd never performed there.

We not only had the opportunity to perform "Shine On Us" with a full orchestra, we got to do it with all of these tremendous artists who were on the album with us. **—Randy, Shawn & Dan**

Lessons from "Shine On Us"

Randy, Shawn & Dan say, "The truth is, it doesn't matter how dark the day, how deep the valley, how painful the depression, the light of Jesus is available to all of us. We know the One who brings light to dark." When has the light of Jesus guided you through a dark time in your life?

_____

_____

_____

_____

_____

_____

The Bible says, "Even the darkness will not be dark to you; the night will shine like the day, for darkness is as light to you" (Ps. 139:12 NIV) What do you think the psalmist means in this verse, and how does it apply to you circumstances?

_____

_____

_____

_____

_____

_____

_____

Mediate on this verse: "Let the light of your face shine upon us, O LORD" (Ps. 4:6NIV).

_____

_____

_____

_____

_____

What is God telling you about this verse? How might it apply to your life?

_____

_____

_____

_____

_____

We Worship God Because He's God
By Shawn Craig

I came from the old school. The worship leader was the "song leader." He would get up and say, "Turn in your hymnals to page 29." The songs we sang were not the classic worshipful hymns like "Crown Him with Many Crowns." They were largely songs about the Christian life and the hope of Heaven. Good songs, but not much vertical worship took place.

Sometime in the mid-80s I experienced a congregation singing the song "I Exalt Thee." I had never seen people worship so passionately. I got it! I saw that the essence of worship should be to worship God because he's God. Period. My motive for leading worship became focused more on God and less on self.

Worship leading is not coercive. It is graceful and interactive with the Holy Spirit.

Worship is not all about you or me. It's about him. Many come to worship saying, "I don't feel like it," or "It's not my nature to respond the way you are prompting me." I want to say, "It's not about what you like; it's about what God likes. God has given us scriptural foundation for the kind of worship and the patterns of praise that he likes." Worship is about him.

This kind of position makes my role as worship leader a subversive one. I'm working against human nature and the selfishness in all of us (myself included!). How do we attempt to change this mindset? With scriptural application along with demonstration by example. I must do what I am asking them to do. Do I ask for humble obedience? Then I must live this in front of those I lead.

A worship lifestyle means different things to different people. For me, it's best summed up in the little book written by Brother Lawrence. He called it "Practicing the Presence." The essence of this idea is that we acknowledge God's Presence daily, then hourly, until at some point in our lifetime it becomes like breathing.

He'll Do Whatever It Takes

Composed by Dan Dean
Album: *Lifeline* (1995)

"Your attitude should be the same as that of Christ Jesus: Who, being in very nature God, did not consider equality with God something to be grasped, but made himself nothing, taking the very nature of a servant, being made in human likeness. And being found in appearance as a man, he humbled himself and became obedient to death—even death on a cross!" (Phil. 2:5–8 NIV)

"You don't know just how far
 Away from home I've been"
 She said, as she looked into my eyes
"Could it be I've strayed beyond
 Mercy's outstretched hand
 And now His grace no longer stoops
 To hear my cry
 You see, I just wanna know
 Tell me how far will He go

Will He still reach for me
In spite of where I've been"
And I told her

Chorus
He'll do whatever, whatever it takes
His grace reaches lower than your worst mistakes
And His love will run farther
Than you can run away, my friend
He'll do whatever, whatever it takes
He'll do whatever it takes

I've heard His love is patient
That He always hears a prayer
And that His love will follow you
Despite the miles
My best years of life I wasted
Why would He even really care
What have I to give
That He would find worthwhile
You see I just wanna know
Tell me how far will He go
Will He still reach for me
In spite of who I am
Let me tell you

Chorus

He'll just keep reaching
Until He finds a way to bring you back
Where you belong
Come on back home

GMA Dove Nomination—Inspirational Album of the Year in 1995

The Story Behind the Song

When Marie* stepped through the doors of my church one Sunday, I knew some of her background already. I knew she had experienced a tough life. Clearly strung out on drugs, she hadn't been in a church in a long time.

When time came for the invitation, I admit I was shocked to see her kneeling at the altar, her make-up running, as tears flowed from her face. When I went to meet her, I told her something preachers often say without thinking, "You know, the Lord loves you."

Clearly doubtful, she looked up at me and said, "Pastor, you don't know where I've been and what I've done. There's no way he could love me."

The Bible promises us that the Holy Spirit will give us the words to say when we need them. God brought to mind a story that I had learned long before from 2 Samuel 14, the interaction between King David and the woman from Tekoa. The woman said to David that the Lord "would devise plans so that the one banished from Him does not remain banished" (v. 14 HCSB). It is a very prophetic verse that reminds us that when there was no way to get to God, he created a way.

I shared that truth with Marie that day. I let her know that nothing she could ever do could take her so low that God's grace couldn't reach her.

For me, it was an unforgettable moment when I got to see God use me in a profound way. But truly it was the first of many "God-moments" with this song.

As we've performed it through the years, I've seen God use it many times to heal the broken. —**Dan**

* Name changed for privacy.

Lessons from "He'll Do Whatever It Takes"

The song lyrics say, "He'll do whatever, whatever it takes. His grace reaches lower than your worst mistakes. And His love will run farther than you can run away . . ." Over and over God shows us that his grace is greater than our sin. How has this biblical truth transformed your life? If it hasn't, ask God to help you believe in his grace today.

_____

_____

_____

_____

_____

_____

Dan says Marie told him: "Pastor, you don't know where I've been and what I've done. There's no way he could love me." How would you explain to Marie that God loves her no matter what? What verses could you use to support your explanation?

_____

The Bible says, "But God does not take away life; instead, he devises ways so that a banished person may not remain estranged from him" (2 Sam. 14:14 NIV). How would you explain this verse to Marie?

"How Can I Know God's Will?"
By Shawn Craig

It's a question I'm asked as a pastor more than any other. I've asked it too. Most of the time, I think this question comes from a good motive. We want to know that our choice pleases God. We want our lives to count and our days to have significance.

But it can also come from a passive stance: maybe the truth is that I want someone else to make the decision for me so I can be off the hook of responsibility. If it doesn't turn out like I thought, I don't have to blame myself. I can chalk one up to "God's choice for me includes suffering." Or, I simply don't want to put the time into seeking wise counsel from people who have walked where I've walked, reading the stories of those who had similar decisions before them, or setting aside the time to seek the Lord and examine my motives in the light of the Scripture and the Holy Spirit.

Without equivocation, I can name one thing for certain that is God's will. It's found in 1 Thessalonians 4:3: "For this is the will of God, your sanctification." The apostle is emphatic here. Know this: God's will is for you to be "made holy." The mission of the Holy Spirit in your life is that your body, your mind, and your spirit are set apart for his purposes. He wants you to glorify God through your vocation, marriage, money, and ministry. This is God's will for you.

I've found it helpful to change my prayer from, "God, what do you want me to do?" to "God, which of these paths will make me more like your Son?" Or, instead of asking,

"God, which path should I take?" ask, "God, which path leads toward glorifying you—toward holiness?"

> Many Christians feel more comfortable with the idea that apart from Christ they can do nothing, than they do with the other side of that coin: that they can do all things through Him who strengthens them. "I can do nothing" lets me off the hook; "I can do all things" makes me wonder why I'm not doing anything. It's easier to piddle around wondering whether it's God's will that you rent this apartment or that one, than it is to face up to God's ultimate will for you: that you become conformed to the image of His Son. (John Boykin in *The Gospel of Coincidence*, 168)

Ouch. I've been there. I've piddled around with that kind of question. Pulling back to ask the larger question is harder and more probing. But here's what I know, and it's one thing that's certain in every decision: I can know, if I am a Christ-follower, that God's desire is that I become a reflection of Jesus.

Imagine how this could shape your decisions regarding:

- Which person should I date?
- Which job should I take?
- Where should we go to church?
- Should I lead a life group

Here's where you can find some clarity: this is God's will, your sanctification.

Build a Bridge of Love

Composed by Jeff Switzer and Randy Phillips
Album: *Lifeline* (1994)

*"We love because he first loved us. If anyone says, 'I
love God,' yet hates his brother, he is a liar. For anyone
who does not love his brother, whom he has seen,
cannot love God, whom he has not seen. And he has
given us this command: Whoever loves God must also
love his brother." (1 John 4:19–21 NIV)*

Isn't it crazy, we haven't spoken in years
We were the closest friends
Where did we part, when did the love disappear
We thought it'd never end
Just a causeless separation
A turn in the road of life
But now we're nothing more than strangers
Don't you think that it's time to

Let's build a bridge of love together
One stone of hope at a time

Let's span the sea that comes between us
So join your hand and heart with mine

The timing is right for our differences to cease
O Father make us one
Let's join in the fight to love all humanity
Our time has just begun
We can use these precious moments
To tear apart dividing walls
And with those stones of separation
Build a bridge for all
Every race and every nation
United and unique
We're all just links in a chain of love
I need you, you need me

GMA Dove Nomination—Inspirational Album of the Year in 1995

The Story Behind the Song

You've probably heard of the Hatfields and McCoys and
the Capulets and Montagues. I had a real-life case of bat-
tling families in one of the churches where I pastored. They

fought, bickered, and struggled over everything. It was incredibly sad.

One of the families ran a successful company that built bridges all over Texas. I remember sitting down with the family one day and trying desperately to come up with an illustration that would help me communicate the importance of healing the rift. Bridges seemed to be a natural, considering the family's career.

My grandpa was also a bridge-builder all through the southeast. I remember him telling me at one point that he could use the same material to either build a bridge or a barrier.

So, as I sat with one of these families, I appealed to that analogy. All the energy they were employing to bicker with one another could be used to do something incredible if they channeled it constructively.

"Would you rather be a barrier-builder or a bridge-builder?" I asked. "Would you rather be right or reconciled?"

In the months that followed that conversation, the relationship began to mend. And in the many years that have come and gone since, the rift between those families has been completely healed by the new generations.

This song was built from that meeting. I wrote this song for any person who has ever faced an ex-spouse, an ex-pastor, or an ex-friend and found themselves so emotionally entrenched in being right that they believe they'll never be able to reconcile.

I hope that anyone who is in a conflict will listen to this song and realize that being reconciled is better. We may not agree with everything the other person says. We may not be able to be friends with those we oppose. But we can refuse to hang on to bitterness. We can choose forgiveness.

We can build a bridge instead of a barrier. —**Randy**

Lessons from "Build a Bridge of Love"

Jesus is the bridge between you and the Father. He is the one Mediator, the only way to God. Think about this bridge of love that spans from God to you as you meditate on this scripture passage:

> But now in Christ Jesus you who once were far away have been brought near through the blood of Christ.
>
> For he himself is our peace, who has made the two one and has destroyed the barrier, the dividing wall of hostility, by abolishing in his flesh the law with its commandments and regulations. His purpose was to create in himself one new man out of the two, thus making peace, and in this one body to reconcile both of them to God through the cross, by which he put to death their hostility.
>
> He came and preached peace to you who were far away and peace to those who were near. For through him we both have access to the Father by one Spirit.
>
> Consequently, you are no longer foreigners and aliens, but fellow citizens with God's people and members of God's household, built on the

foundation of the apostles and prophets, with Christ Jesus himself as the chief cornerstone.

In him the whole building is joined together and rises to become a holy temple in the Lord. And in him you too are being built together to become a dwelling in which God lives by his Spirit. (Eph. 2:13–22 NIV)

What is God telling you about this passage? How might it apply to your life?

_____

_____

_____

_____

_____

_____

_____

_____

_____

_____

Growing Together

For most of my life the view of the Body of Christ has been so limited. Touring across the United States has changed that. We've performed in just about every state in the country. Doing so has opened up my eyes to the diversity and scope of the Body of Christ. —**Randy**

God has used my past twenty-five years of experience with Phillips, Craig & Dean to expand my vision of the Body of Christ. When I was growing up, I found myself in a pond that I thought was pretty big. I had a picture of what I thought the Body of Christ looked like. We started going across the country and visiting other churches, and my vision just swelled to what I think the Body of Christ really looks like—an innumerable cloud of witnesses. I believe it's much bigger than any of us typically imagine.

Plus, being around each other has been incredible for me. Iron sharpens iron. Shawn is one of the most disciplined people I know. I admire his discipline in everything from his personal study habits to his eating habits to exercise and beyond. Knowing Shawn has challenged me to become more disciplined.

Randy, on the other hand, is an incredible visionary. He always sees good, always sees growth opportunities. He is one of the most positive people I've ever been around. There probably wouldn't be a Phillips, Craig & Dean without his vision.

Finally, when you've spent twenty-five years watching God use you in ways you had never dreamed, it changes you. When you hear the stories, it really allows you to see how God can use you as you remain pliable and you hear his voice. **—Dan**

Just like anyone else, we have ups and downs in our relationship with Christ. At times we feel very close to him. Other times he feels further away, and the Christian life seems more difficult.

First, it has given me a greater appreciation for the wider Body of Christ. We've met so many people who share the basic tenets of the Christian faith and with whom we have so much in common. What we hold in an open hand doesn't have to divide us. Before Phillips, Craig & Dean, I don't think I understood how beautiful are all the different tribes and streams that come together in this wonderful Body that Jesus died for, the Church.

Second, the partnership we've shared has grown me and sanctified me. As in a marriage, you start out thinking that you're going to change the other person. When you're together frequently, the little things that make us unique can drive one another crazy. We were no exception that. By God's grace, we've stuck it out. We learned pretty quickly that some of the things that drive us crazy about each other are strengths in the other person that God uses to grow us.

We've learned to lean in on each other's strengths. Where one person is weak, the other is often strong.

We have a very similar humor, but we have a lot of differences, too.

Early in our ministry together, someone asked us how we'd each react to seeing someone down-and-out on the side of the road. We'd each react very differently, but we complement one another.

Dan would get down in the ditch and cry with the person. I'd give them ten steps on how to get back on their feet. Randy would tell them, "Get up and get going," and give them a big kick in the pants.

I know I don't have all the answers. I need the strengths of the other guys. We lean on each other. We're meant to complement one another. We have to persevere in love and accept one another's faults—and look at our own. We can't give up on each other. **—Shawn**

I Want to Be Just Like You

Composed by Dan Dean and Joy Becker
Album: *Lifeline* (1994)

*"Whoever claims to live in him must walk as Jesus did"
(1 John 2:6 NIV).*

He climbs in my lap for a goodnight hug
He calls me Dad and I call him Bub
With his faded old pillow and a bear named Pooh
He snuggles up close and says "I want to be like you"
I tuck him in bed and I kiss him goodnight
Trippin' over the toys as I turn out the light
And I whisper a prayer that someday he'll see
He's got a Father in God 'cause he's seen Jesus in me

Chorus
Lord, I want to be just like You
'Cause he wants to be just like me
I want to be a holy example
For his innocent eyes to see
Help me be a living Bible, Lord

That my little boy can read
I want to be just like You
'Cause he wants to be like me

Got to admit I've got so far to go
Make so many mistakes and I'm sure that You know
Sometimes it seems no matter how hard I try
With all the pressures in life I just can't get it all right
But I'm trying so hard to learn from the best
Being patient and kind, filled with Your tenderness
'Cause I know that he'll learn from the things that he sees
And the Jesus he finds will be the Jesus in me

Repeat chorus

Right now from where he stands I may seem mighty tall
But it's only 'cause I'm learning from the best Father of
them all

Repeat chorus

GMA Dove Nomination—Inspirational Song of the Year, 1995
GMA Dove Nomination—Inspirational Album of the Year, 1995

The Story Behind the Song

My fourteen-year-old son, Dusty, and I went to a teen camp some years back. I didn't realize it, but Dusty brought along a pair of my shoes—two sizes too big for him.

On Saturday evening of the camp, families joined the teens for activities, and then they split us up into small groups. A facilitator asked my son why he brought my shoes with him that weekend.

Dusty's answer led me to tears. He talked about how much he wanted to be like me. Although I had co-written this song a few years earlier, the truth of the lyrics hit home in a new way.

As parents, we have such a unique opportunity to model the Fatherhood of God to the children whom he has entrusted to us.

Children have an innate desire to be like their parents. Built into that is the desire to emulate the greatest passions of their parents' lives. If a parent loves sports, often the child will too. If the parent loves money, often so will the child.

It makes sense that if the parent loves Jesus—more than anything else—there's a good chance the child will too someday.

We can get so much of our picture of who God is by looking at our earthly father.

So many people have bad pictures of God because their earthly fathers have shown them bad models. I love to see dads who have made the decision to break the cycle of brokenness and become the kind of men their children can emulate,, dads who are willing to pray, "Lord, I want to be just like you, because he wants to be just like me."

That's a hero in my book.

Over and over again, we've had fathers tell us how this song has challenged them to be better fathers to their children. Many have told us how they'll hear the song on the radio and have to pull over because tears filled their eyes. That's why we do what we do as Christian artists. We long to see God change the lives of people through our music. We've seen it over and over through this song.

Many people don't realize that Joy Becker, who helped shape many of the words that make up this song, doesn't have children—or that she was orphaned when she was thirteen. A woman who had very little personal knowledge of parenting shaped the words of a song that has helped a generation of parents turn their eyes to God to find a model of biblical parenting. **—Dan**

A few years back, I hired a contractor to build our house. Although I didn't know the contractor beforehand, the contractor knew me. As we were ready to sign on the dotted, the contractor told me: "I have to tell you. I listened to 'I Want to Be Just Like You' almost every night for years with my three boys. It has become a theme song for us." His kids were away at school, so he was getting choked up as he talked about it.

He didn't want to tell me ahead of time because he feared I'd think he was trying to use the connection to make the sale. But as I've gotten to know him over the years, I've discovered that his love for Jesus is real. **—Shawn**

I'll never forget one particular family who came up to talk with us after a concert. They told us how this song played an important part in their relationship with their son at two different pivotal times. The first time had been during a time of great joy. The dad had sung "I Want to Be Just Like You" at the boy's dedication. Their son was born after they had hoped and prayed for a long time that God would give them a child.

Yet the second time this song played a powerful part in their lives was a few years later at the boy's funeral. Their son had gone home to be with Jesus at a much younger age than they expected. On the day they celebrated the boy's life, they sang "I Want to be Just Like You" at his funeral.

God used this song to minister to this family during the two bookends of his life. **—Shawn**

It's hard to have an intimate moment with fifty thousand guys, but I'll never forget singing "I Want to Be Just Like You" at Promise Keepers rallies in the 1990s. There's just something about those lyrics. Whenever we'd sing this song, it would get so eerily quiet. It was like the souls of men were absorbing the depth of the lyrics. It was something pretty special. Men would come up to us afterwards and tell us that when they got home they'd be better fathers. —**Randy**

Lessons from "I Want to Be Just Like You"

The song lyrics say, "Help me be a living Bible, Lord." What would your life look like if you were a living Bible?

_____

_____

_____

_____

_____

_____

_____

_____

What changes could you make in your life to be more of a living Bible?

_____

_____

_____

_____

_____

What do you think about this statement from Dan Dean: "It makes sense that if the parent loves Jesus—more than anything else—there's a good chance the child will too someday."

"Your attitude should be the same as that of Christ Jesus: Who, being in very nature God, did not consider equality with God something to be grasped, but made himself nothing, taking the very nature of a servant, being made in human likeness" (Phil. 2:5–7 NIV).

Concert of the Age

Composed by Geoff Thurman and Jeoffrey Benward
Album: *Lifeline* (1994)

*"I saw a huge crowd, too huge to count. Everyone was
there—all nations and tribes, all races and languages.
And they were standing, dressed in white robes and
waving palm branches, standing before the Throne
and the Lamb and heartily singing: Salvation to our
God on his Throne! Salvation to the Lamb!*

*"All who were standing around the Throne—
Angels, Elders, Animals—fell on their faces before
the Throne and worshiped God, singing: Oh, Yes! The
blessing and glory and wisdom and thanksgiving,
The honor and power and strength, To our God
forever and ever and ever! Oh, Yes!" (Rev. 7:9–13 The
Message).*

The stars become as lasers
And all the worlds align
Horizon to horizon
A rainbow begins to rise

Sudden sounds like thunder
Come from everywhere
As the angel Michael
Kicks the countdown on the snare

Across the sea of faces
Shouts of praise begin to roll
As we see the silhouette
Of the King of heart and soul

At the concert of the age
The great I AM takes center stage
The generations stand amazed
At the concert of the age

Then a voice like a trumpet
Blows through me like the wind
Gabriel cries, "Welcome home,
We're ready to begin"

We know you heard Beethoven
And the king of rock-n-roll
But on behalf of the Father
We give you the King of heart and soul
At the concert of the age
The great I AM takes center stage
The generations stand amazed
At the concert of the age

At the concert of the age
The great I AM takes center stage
The generations stand amazed
At the concert of the age

We cry Holy, holy, holy,
Lord God Almighty
With every note He plays

At the concert of the age
The great I AM takes center stage
The generations stand amazed
At the concert of the age

GMA Dove Nomination—Inspirational Album of the Year (1995)

The Story Behind the Song

If we're honest, most Christian artists can recite times growing up when we've dreamed of great concerts in front of throngs of people. We hope those dreams aren't selfish ambitions to boost our own egos, but we recognize that at times they are.

This song by Geoff Thurman and Jeoffrey Benward reminds us that our focus as musicians can't be on ourselves. As musicians who seek to honor the Lord, we're not called to be the star of the show.

We're called to point others to the Star of the Show.

When you attend a highly anticipated concert, there's one moment that stands head and shoulders above all the rest—it's the time when the star takes center stage.

As great as that moment can be during a concert, it's nothing compared to another moment that God has been preparing for us since the foundation of the world.

There will come a day when this age will be done. We'll gather around the throne of God, and the Lamb of God will be revealed in all his glory. What will that moment sound like? What will it feel like?

That's what the "Concert of the Age" is all about. It's a song that sought to illustrate the revelation of Christ as a concert performance. It particularly highlights the coming of the King as the Star of the Show.

When we started to work on our second album, *Lifeline*, we turned to a songwriter that had given us one of our best hits of the first album, *Turn Up the Radio*. We asked Geoff Thurman if he had any other songs like that. At that point we were experimenting with some new pop sounds—an earthy sound mixed with church vocals.

Geoff showed us "Concert of the Age." It became one of the most requested singles of our career. We've always enjoyed singing it. In fact, for many years we've ended our concerts with this song. We wanted to remind those who came to our concerts that although we had a great time together, it doesn't compare to what is in store for us when Jesus returns. —**Randy, Shawn, and Dan**

Lessons from "Concert of the Age"

Randy, Shawn, and Dan say, "There will come a day when this age will be done. We'll gather around the throne of God and the Lamb of God will be revealed in all of his glory." How does seeing this picture of eternity help you set priorities today?

The song lyrics say, "But on behalf of the Father, we give you the King of heart and soul . . ." What do you think the phrase/title "King of heart and soul" means? Why should we bow down to the King of heart and soul?

_____

_____

_____

_____

_____

_____

_____

_____

_____

_____

Say this as a prayer:

> *"Great and marvelous are your works, O Lord God, the Almighty. Just and true are your ways, O King of the nations. Who will not fear you, Lord, and glorify your name? For you alone are holy. All nations will come and worship before you, for your righteous deeds have been revealed" (Rev. 15:3–4 NLT).*

Supernatural Singing
By Shawn Craig

Songs move us. my youngest brother Bryson proved it. When he was about a year old or less, we discovered that if we sang certain songs he would pucker up. I thought this was cool! I used to line up my buddies, and I would sing a couple of lines and say, "Watch this." Sure enough, as I sang, out would go his lip! Songs move us.

Songs go deeper than thought. They touch the heart. History reveals it. We know it's true. That's why the earliest military endeavors included songs and music as a part of war. They learned that when spirits were low and the outlook was bleak, a couple of drums and a flute could lift the spirits. Hope could be restored. It's why virtually every nation and kingdom has a national anthem. It inspires pride and hope.

Who hasn't at some point in their life got a lump in their throat when the flag passed by and they sang "The Star-Spangled Banner"? It's why high schools have marching bands, and smart marketing ads use music. Songs move us.

But with Christians, it's even bigger than this. Songs as worship to God can actually change the atmosphere. A quick read of Acts 16 will prove it. Imagine Paul and Silas, beaten, bloody, chained up in a cell.

And these cells didn't have A/C and a TV like ours today. They were dark, dank,gloomy places. But what did Paul and Silas decide to do at midnight? Sing and glorify God. I can imagine Paul saying to Silas, "Okay, Silas. We've prayed. We've prayed some more. We've talked and witnessed to these guards. What now? How about singing?"

So they do, and God hears their singing, and the walls begin to shake, and the chains fall off, and soon revival breaks out! The head guard and his family are baptized. And so the church at Philippi grows as Jesus uses a couple of guys singing praise in a jail cell!

No, it's not magic, and not everyone who is in a crisis can sing their way out. But before you say, "God doesn't do that anymore," don't discount it either. Praise still paves the way for God's supernatural intervention.

Are you in a prison of doubt? Of discouragement? Of temptation? Of hopelessness? Ramp up the praise. Perhaps God will use that as an opportunity to break in and loose the chains on your soul.

Turn Up the Radio

Composed by Geoffrey P. Thurman
Album: *Phillips, Craig & Dean* (1992)

"Rejoice, you Gentiles, with His people!

"And again: Praise the Lord, all you Gentiles; all the peoples should praise Him!

"And again, Isaiah says: The root of Jesse will appear, the One who rises to rule the Gentiles; the Gentiles will hope in Him.

"Now may the God of hope fill you with all joy and peace as you believe [in Him] so that you may overflow with hope by the power of the Holy Spirit" (Rom. 15:10–13 HCSB).

I've been kind of down today
Kind of like I can't quite make it
The pressure of a fast-track world
Is hard to handle now and then

I haven't got a lot to say
And I've resolved that I won't take it anymore
I know that somethin' good is movin' in me

That's when I feel the music
Soothe the savage beast
I hear the love, I find release

Chorus
Turn up the radio
And sing a song of sympathy
Turn up the radio
Let freedom ring in harmony
I hear the healing go
To the secret place only God can know
Turn up the radio!
Turn up the Radio!

Don't you know I make mistakes?
And I can surely feel forsaken
The pressure of a fast-paced race
Hurts my already broken Heart

When the road is headed down and out
And I desire love's forgiveness
His Spirit calls my name again and again
That's when I feel His music
Soothe the savage beast
I hear my Lord, I find His peace

Chorus

Let a message of hope sink in
Feel a fire of life begin

Break out of the chains
Sing a sweet refrain

The Story Behind the Song

When we were first introduced to this song, it didn't seem like a fit for us. We were recording our very first album. We were still green around the ears and just discovering what our sound would be.

"Turn Up the Radio" didn't have much of a spiritual message to it. It was a fun, catchy pop song that our record label insisted we include. In our minds, every song had to be a ministry song. We didn't want to waste our time with a song that didn't have a strong message. We were three church boys. We understood the inspirational music world. We knew much less about the contemporary Christian music scene. If we couldn't perform it from our church platforms, we didn't want to include it on our albums. This song wouldn't touch anybody. We were sure of that.

We had started to develop a relationship with smaller inspirational radio stations. We wanted them to respect us. We were sure that this catchy pop song would have the opposite effect. They wouldn't play our music ever again— or so we thought.

To our total surprise, this song took off. God chose this song to create a ministry platform that we've enjoyed for twenty-five years now. It was the first single we ever released—and it soared to Number One.

This was truly the song that started our ministry. Dan tells the story of waking up one morning to "Turn Up the Radio" on his alarm clock. In his excitement of hearing us on the radio, he called Randy and asked, "Do you know what this is? It's us on the radio!"

This song also became the subject of one of our biggest mistakes as a young group. We had been invited to sing at a Bill Gaither Praise Gathering. Jackie Patillo, our A & R director at the time, told us we had three songs to sing—and one had to be "Turn Up the Radio."

"No way," we said. "This isn't the place for that song."

"You're going to sing this song," she said. "This is the song that's putting you on the map."

We still didn't buy it. We went behind her back and agreed not to do it.

It was a huge mistake. We walked off the stage and looked at Jackie. She had steam coming out of her ears. We learned a valuable lesson that evening—especially after Bill Gaither asked, "Why didn't you guys do that 'radio' song?"

Do what Jackie says. —**Randy, Shawn, & Dan**

Lessons from "Turn Up the Radio"

The song lyrics say, "His Spirit calls my name again and again that's when I feel His music."

Meditate on this passage—

> Therefore, since we have been declared righteous by faith, we have peace with God through our Lord Jesus Christ.
>
> We have also obtained access through Him by faith into this grace in which we stand, and we rejoice in the hope of the glory of God. And not only that, but we also rejoice in our afflictions, because we know that affliction produces endurance, endurance produces proven character, and proven character produces hope.
>
> This hope will not disappoint [us], because God's love has been poured out in our hearts through the Holy Spirit who was given to us. (Rom. 5:1–5 HCSB)

What is God telling you about this passage? How might it apply to your life?

Behind the Scenes with
Phillips, Craig & Dean

I'm the only blond in the group—blond mixed with a little gray. I've been asked why my name is last, and I say the Bible says "the last shall be first."

When we first got together, there was debate about names and if we should use our names or create a new name. I remember one of the record company execs saying, "You need something that feels like 'Crosby, Stills and Nash,'" so I really think they looked at the feel rather than the sequence. It just rolled off the tongue better that way. But again, knowing Randy, he might have had something to do with this, a little payoff money on the side. **—Dan Dean**

My memories of recording sessions contain both agony and fun. I can remember in the early days recording in Paul Mills' converted garage—in a tiny bathroom with a washer and dryer in it. In the middle of the summer and roasting, we were huddled around one microphone. Paul had to turn off the air conditioner because of the noise. When we'd get too hot, Paul would tell us to come out of the bathroom, and we'd turn on his air conditioner.

Or, I'll never forget the time we were all huddled around a single microphone for hours trying to nail a chorus. Today we can all sing separately and they can put our tracks together. That wasn't true when we first got started. After hours of doing this, we were ready to go after the next person who jangled keys in his pocket—all in good fun, of course.

I've also experienced those meltdown moments on solos when the producer has asked me to keep trying to get the song right. Over and over I'd do it until I thought I couldn't do it again. Then I'd try again. Eventually, I'd get it right. **—Shawn**

On the road, we eat breakfast together each day we record. We discuss the previous recording session and what went well and what we can improve on. We have supper together as well. It is here that we will laugh about funny moments in the studio and our favorite memories of past years. **—Randy Phillips**

Over the years, we've collected key chains. We connected them all together, and now we play this game of tag "you're it" with the biggest key chain you've ever seen. It ends up in your luggage, and you have to get rid of it. It shows up at the oddest times and in the oddest places. **—Shawn Craig**

We were singing in Parkersburg, West Virginia. It was a very large, boisterous crowd that was ready to have some fun. At the end of the second or third song, a young lady rushed the stage. I was thinking, "Wow, I've never had this happen before." Then I heard her say in the most unobtrusive way possible, "Your pants are unzipped." **—Dan Dean**

During a time of worship, I started to lead a song one time and had a brain freeze. There were two songs that had similar words. I couldn't get the other melody out of my head. I finally gave up after a few lines and said, "Let's try something else!" Learning not to take yourself too seriously in such situations is an important step. —**Shawn Craig**

Favorite Song of All

Composed by Dan Dean
Album: Phillips, *Craig & Dean* (1992)

*"In the same way, there is more joy in heaven over one
lost sinner who repents and returns to God than over
ninety-nine others who are righteous and haven't
strayed away!" (Luke 15:7 NLT).*

He loves to hear the wind sing
as it whistles through the pines on mountain peaks
And He loves to hear the raindrops
as they splash to the ground in a magic melody
He smiles in sweet approval
as the waves crash through the rocks in harmony
And creation joins in unity
to sing to Him majestic symphonies

But His favorite song of all
Is the song of the redeemed
When lost sinners now made clean
Lift their voices loud and strong

When those purchased by His blood
Lift to Him a song of love
There's nothin' more He'd rather hear
Nor so pleasin' to His ear
As His favorite song of all

And He loves to hear the angels
as they sing, "Holy, holy is the Lamb"
Heaven's choirs in harmony
lift up praises to the Great I Am
But He lifts His hands for silence
when the weakest saved by grace begins to sing
And a million angels listen
as a newborn soul sings, "I've been redeemed!"

'Cause His favorite song of all
Is the song of the redeemed
When lost sinners now made clean
Lift their voices loud and strong
When those purchased by His blood
Lift to Him a song of love
There's nothin' more He'd rather hear
Nor so pleasin' to His ear
As His favorite song of all

It's not just melodies and harmonies
That catches His attention
It's not just clever lines and phrases

That causes Him to stop and listen
But when anyone set free,
Washed and bought by Calvary begins to sing

That's His favorite song of all
Is the song of the redeemed
When lost sinners now made clean
Lift their voices loud and strong
When those purchased by His blood
Lift to Him a song of love
There's nothin' more He'd rather hear
Nor so pleasin' to His ear
As His favorite song of all

Holy, holy, holy is the Lamb
Halleluiah, halleluiah

No. 1 Song of the Year (*CCM Magazine*, 1993)

The Story Behind the Song

When I first wrote this song close to thirty years ago now,
churches often had what we called all-night concerts
(although they didn't last all night). The evening would

be full of different kinds of musical acts—from choirs to Gospel to Southern Gospel to the beginnings of Christian rap. One evening as I listened to the different acts, I began wondering what type of music God loves best.

Around that same time, I went on my first skiing trip. I'll never forget that amazing opportunity to see God's creation front and center. While I was on that trip, I realized that all of nature—from the wind whistling through the trees to the birds chirping—sings a song to God. Nature's song beautifully brings honor to the Lord.

Yet as I thought about the different musical styles at that all-night concert and the natural music I could hear during my skiing trip, I came to the realization that God's favorite song wasn't any of those choices.

Instead God favors the simple song of the redeemed. The Bible tells us that all of heaven rejoices when one sinner repents. Nothing pleases the heart of God more than one person accepting his free offer of grace. It's music to the heart of our Creator. I hoped to bring attention to that truth through this song.

As much as I appreciated the message behind this song, I had my doubts about whether it would really resonate with others. I usually try out a new song with my home congregation before I share it as a possibility with Randy and Shawn. When I shared this song with my congregation, it seemed like a flop. When it came time to record our first album, I was reticent to include it.

Even after deciding to include it, I continued to harbor doubts. In fact, if you listen to the initial recording, you'll hear me mutter at the beginning, "I love you, Jesus." Of course, that was obviously an affirmation of something I certainly believe, but it was also a prayer for help. I wasn't sure how this song would go.

When we released that first album, our producer included that simple prayer at the beginning.

We were about to perform on "The 700 Club" in Virginia Beach, Viginia., when we first learned that the song—which was the second single we released off that first album—had become the Number One song in the country. Remembering my early trepidation about the song, I was astounded but very grateful.

Over time this became a special song for our group. It's the first song we sang together as a group. To know that thousands of people were listening to the song and worship leaders were leading congregations to sing it together was a thrilling ride for us.

—Dan

Lessons from "Favorite Song of All"

The song lyrics say, "But His favorite song of all Is the song of the redeemed When lost sinners now made clean Lift their voices loud and strong When those purchased by His blood Lift to Him a song of love There's nothin' more He'd rather hear." Why is the song of the redeemed so precious to God? How much did it cost God to offer us redemption?

_____

_____

_____

_____

_____

_____

_____

_____

_____

_____

_____

_____

_____

The Bible says, "In the same way, there is more joy in heaven over one lost sinner who repents and returns to God than over ninety-nine others who are righteous and haven't strayed away!" (Luke 15:7 NLT). Rick Warren says this means we serve a Party God. Does knowing that God loves a party, particularly when it involves the redeemed, change the way you think of God?

Midnight Oil

Composed by Joy Becker and Shawn Craig
Album: *Phillips, Craig & Dean* (1992)

*"Be persistent in prayer, and keep alert as you pray,
giving thanks to God"* (Col. 4:2TEV).

Mama always got up early
And she never went to bed 'til late
Yet, I never heard her complainin'
About her family of eight
There were times she should have been sleepin'
But, late in the midnight hour
She'd get down on her knees
And you could hear her say,
"Lord fill them with your power"

Chorus
Mama liked to burn the midnight oil
Down on her knees in prayer
If you asked why she did it
She said she did it 'cause she cared

Now Mama knew that Jesus was waitin'
When she knelt by her rocking chair
Oh, I'm glad my mama was willin'
To burn the midnight oil in prayer

Now Mama's gone to be with Jesus
I've got a family of my own
Yet, whenever the clock strikes midnight
You will find me all alone
That's when I start to call upon Jesus
For His wisdom and His power
'Cause it seems that He loves
To hear a Daddy's prayer
Even in the midnight hour

Chorus
Years from now, when my grown little boy
Has a family of his own
Will he kneel down and pray
When the hour is late
And pass the legacy on

Chorus

'Cause now there's a Daddy who's willing
To burn the midnight oil in prayer

The Story Behind the Song

When Joy Becker first came to me with this song more than twenty-five years ago, it immediately resonated with me.

Just like the man in the song, I too had a praying mother (and a praying father for that matter), although I can't say I ever remember my mom on her knees at actual midnight.

First of all, we weren't allowed to be up that late! Second, my mom wasn't a night owl, but she certainly was a woman of prayer. I remember her faithfulness to attend the Tuesday morning prayer meeting at our small church. When she'd come home, I'd see the red nose and red eyes and know she'd been crying as she prayed for our family—and others.

As a child, you take a praying mother for granted, but as I've grown older, I've begun to treasure it. I'll never forget one birthday when she sent me a card that said in it: "I'm not sending you a gift this year. Instead, I went by the church today and spent an hour in prayer for you." That's an amazing gift for any mother to give. So when Joy shared this song with me, I immediately thought of my mom.

Joy impressed me with this song from the beginning. She had no children, and her parents had died years ago when she was just thirteen. I was amazed that she would write a song like "Midnight Oil," with such depth about the experience of parenting.

This song played a unique part in the history of Phillips, Craig & Dean. When we started the group in 1991, we each brought one song and promised five thousand dollars if necessary to the new venture. "Midnight Oil" was my contribution.

It became one of our favorites on the first album, and I think it helped define our sound. We each had different musical interests. Being from Texas, Randy and Dan leaned more toward country. I tended to lean more toward contemporary Christian music. For instance, the Imperials, the Second Chapter of Acts, and Keith Green were among my biggest musical influences.

But the three songs we started with helped to shape the future of our group, because it focused us on an earthy sound that came out of church vocals, where you sing the parts in parallel motion.

That became our signature sound. —**Shawn**

Lessons from "Midnight Oil"

The Bible says, "Be persistent in prayer" (Rom. 12:12 HCSB). How can you be more persistent in prayer? Who can you be praying for, like the mother in "Midnight Oil"?

_____

_____

_____

_____

_____

_____

_____

_____

Has there been, or is there, someone praying fervently for you? What has been the effects of that person's prayers for you? Make a point of thanking that person this week.

_____

_____

_____

Shawn says, "I'll never forget one birthday when [my mother] sent me a card that said in it: ;I'm not sending you a gift this year. Instead, I went by the church today and spent an hour in prayer for you.'" What an amazing gift! Think of someone, or several people, who need this gift and commit to giving it to him or her on their birthdays.

Our Songwriting Ministry

The songs we write are an expression of what God is doing in our own souls. It doesn't just happen in a vacuum. I think people understand particular songs when they hear them because the human experience is the same everywhere. We have these experiences that we all walk through that bond us together as humans. Brokenness—and how God intervenes in the midst of it—is one of those experiences.
—Randy

A good song can happen in an instant. You've heard the saying, "There's nothing new under the sun." That's true. You'll never write anything that's never been covered, but God gives certain people the ability to write something that's been written many times in a new way that's never been done before.

It's all about the hook. If you get that hook, the rest will come. I've learned that from some of the best writers in Nashville. You walk around from day to day very sensitive. You can get that hook at any point. You've got to be looking, though.

So much of what I write—of those key ideas—comes from my experience of pastoring the church where God has me and from what is happening in the lives of those I shepherd. A great example of this is the song, "I Choose to Believe." At the time I wrote that, we had several experiences in our church of people who were struggling to believe in

God through tough times such as sickness, unplanned preg-
nancies, and financial difficulties. The song was birthed out
of an attempt to help those people believe in God during
the times when they couldn't see or hear his voice. —**Dan**

What we find as pastors and as singers is that so many
people have had the wind knocked out of them. Abuse,
divorce, listlessness, financial issues, loneliness, betrayal,
health issues—so many things can knock the breath out
of you. How do you breathe in his goodness again, so that
you're not just existing, but living? —**Randy Phillips**

"I think all the songs we write are part of the experiences
that we go through day to day with our church people. I can
look back over the course of a number of albums and see
particular songs that were inspired by something at church
or by a message I heard at a church service. Other songs are
just stuff you live every day. I would say that ninety percent
of the things we write are born out of our experiences going
through life as pastors." —**Dan Dean**

Little Bit of Morning

Composed by Dwight Liles and Randy Phillips
Album: *Phillips, Craig & Dean* (1992)

*"The true light that gives light to every man was
coming into the world" John 1:9 (NIV).*

You can't believe that a night could be
So long and cold
A buried dream, a goal unreached
You've lost your hope

And your will to try is covered by
A full eclipse of the heart
Though your faith is low, still the embers glow
Dreams can live from one small spark

There's a little bit of morning outside
There's a new beginning in the sky
It's been awhile, but now the time is right
To spread your wings and fly

Silent heart, sing a brand new song
The darkest night is just before the dawn
Weary soul arise, wipe the pain from your eyes
There's a little bit of morning outside

The hope He brought seemed all but lost
When they laid Him in the tomb
The dreams, the plans, the healing hands
Wrapped in death and gloom

But early Sunday morn the promise was reborn
At the breaking of the day
He was alive and well, he conquered death and hell
Because He lives now we can say

There's a little bit of morning outside
There's a new beginning in the sky
It's been awhile, but now the time is right
To spread your wings and fly

Silent heart, sing a brand new song
The darkest night is just before the dawn
Weary soul arise, wipe the pain from your eyes
There's a little bit of morning outside, oh yeah

Though the darkness for a moment
May hide tomorrow's light
Just beyond what eyes can see
The light of hope is bright

There's a little bit of morning outside
There's a new beginning in the sky
It's been awhile, but now the time is right
To spread your wings and fly

Silent heart, sing a brand new song
The darkest night is just before the dawn
Weary soul arise, wipe the pain from your eyes
There's a little bit of morning outside, yes it is
Weary soul arise, wipe the pain from your eyes
There's a little bit of morning outside

Weary soul arise, wipe the pain from your eyes
There's a little bit of morning outside
There's a little bit of morning outside
There's a little bit of morning outside
Spread your wings and fly

The Story Behind the Song

If you've ever had a child with colic, you know it's a gift that
keeps on giving. My daughter experienced an awful bout of
it for the first year of life. Every day we dreaded the coming

of night because it was miserable for our daughter and for us. As parents, we longed to be able to comfort her, but we were powerless to do so.

Although her colic got better during the second year, her sleep patterns were already disrupted. It became a habit for her to wake up at certain hours of the night. She still didn't sleep well even into her third year.

We lived on very little sleep. There's a reason why sleep deprivation is a key torture technique. Going to work each day on three hours of sleep will make you consistently miserable. By the time my daughter was three years old, we were beginning to wonder if a normal night of sleep would ever be a part of our lives again.

At three, my daughter could now talk, and we could try to reason with her. One night, as I put her to bed, I whispered, "Please, sleep all night. Don't get up until morning." She responded sweetly, "Okay."

I then went back to sleep, fully expecting to be up in a few hours with her.

Early, early the next morning (I think it was still dark outside), I woke to a tapping on my shoulder. I opened my eyes to see my daughter standing there smiling.

I said, "Sweetheart, I told you not to get up until morning."

She said, "But look, dad," as she pointed to the window, "there's a little bit of morning outside!"

When I told my dad about that experience, he suggested there might be a song in that phrase.

He was right. Life has a way of hitting us hard. One day, all is fine. We're sailing along in the best of spirits. Then someone flips the switch and we're immersed in darkness. We get bad news—divorce papers, a cancer diagnosis, a pink slip at work. Our lives are now as bad as they once were good. As darkness surrounds us, we begin to wonder whether we'll ever see light again. The Bible calls it a night season. And you never know exactly when it'll be over.

That's what it must have been like for the first followers of Jesus on Saturday of resurrection week. With Jesus in the grave, all their hopes and dreams were dashed.

> The hope He brought seemed all but lost
> When they laid Him in the tomb
> The dreams, the plans, the healing hands
> Wrapped in death and gloom

But like us, morning came to Jesus's followers. The Bible says that "at dawn on the first day of the week" a resurrected Jesus showed himself. God doesn't need much light to chase away the darkness. Through the empty tomb, the Lord showed us once and for all that a "little bit of morning" can change history forever.

That means that no matter how dark our days look, we can be confident that we'll see a "little bit of morning" soon. —**Randy**

Lessons from a "Little Bit of Morning"

Describe a time when things were dark, and then God showed a "Little Bit of Morning" into your life?

_____

_____

_____

_____

_____

Meditate upon this Scripture passage:

> After the Sabbath, at dawn on the first day of the week, Mary Magdalene and the other Mary went to look at the tomb.
>
> There was a violent earthquake, for an angel of the Lord came down from heaven and, going to the tomb, rolled back the stone and sat on it. His appearance was like lightning, and his clothes were white as snow.
>
> The guards were so afraid of him that they shook and became like dead men.
>
> The angel said to the women, "Do not be afraid, for I know that you are looking for Jesus,

who was crucified. He is not here; he has risen, just as he said. Come and see the place where he lay. Then go quickly and tell his disciples: 'He has risen from the dead and is going ahead of you into Galilee. There you will see him.' Now I have told you."

So the women hurried away from the tomb, afraid yet filled with joy, and ran to tell his disciples.

Suddenly Jesus met them. "Greetings," he said. They came to him, clasped his feet and worshiped him. Then Jesus said to them, "Do not be afraid. Go and tell my brothers to go to Galilee; there they will see me." (Matt. 28:1–10 NIV)

What is God telling you about this passage? How might it apply to your life?

Little Bit of Morning: *Testimony*

Your songs have been there for so many different seasons of my life but two that stand out are "Little Bit of Morning" because my mother passed away from an extended illness just before dawn on January 31, 1991 and this song went through my mind immediately—silent heart, sing a brand new song, the darkest night is just before the dawn, weary soul arise, wipe the pain from your eyes, there's a little bit of morning outside!

More recently at a concert, you told the story behind and sang the song "Tell Your Heart To Beat Again." My husband had just gone through some heart testing that very day and we drove from there over to the concert. He felt very much like he received healing during that song, and test results the following week confirmed it.

God bless your ministry as you continue to see lives changed through your music. Celebrating with you for 25 blessed years ! —Janet CF

Dan Dean's Battle with Cancer

I went to the doctor for my annual test that I do every year. Never in my wildest dreams did I think I would have some kind of negative response. When I got the call, I said, "My wife is here, do you mind if I put her on speaker?" Then he started telling me the test results were positive for cancer, and for probably thirty or forty minutes he walked through all of the scenarios—what could be, and I did not hear a lot of that at that moment. It was pretty devastating.

My first thought after hearing the news was, "I probably won't ever be able to get any more life insurance." But, of course, sharing the news with my kids was a hard thing to do. My wife was very strong, especially while I was going through my anxiety the first week or so. Then the reality of it set in, and she started having some moments of emotional struggle.

I first called our manager and told him that I'd had the biopsy and that it had come out positive, and I didn't know exactly what was going to happen regarding traveling. At that point I didn't know what treatment I was going to choose, and I thought I wouldn't tell Randy or Shawn, but Chris prevailed and said, "You've got to tell these guys. They would want to know and need to be praying for you. And the churches need to be praying for you." He was right, so I made the call and tried to downplay it and say it was no big deal. But of course it was a big deal! Any time you find out you have cancer, it's a big deal.

As a pastor, my initial thoughts were that I wasn't going to tell the church. I didn't want the drama that this would bring. I didn't want to cause any alarm. I figured I would take a leave of absence or something. But I had several friends who said, "You have to tell the church and share with them, because they are your family. They need to know so they can pray for you." The pastor of Prestonwood Baptist Church, Jack Graham, had the same surgery about two or three years before I did, and I had the opportunity to talk to him about this. Pastor Graham said I would rob my church of the ability to pray for me if I didn't tell them, and that would be a huge mistake. That also helped me to know I had to share with my church.

It was difficult. You don't want to lose your composure. You want to act like you've got things together, not get up there and act like a basket case. Yet it's very emotional to share that kind of news. As you can imagine, they were extremely compassionate, with a great outpouring of support before, during, after, and still.

There's a score with prostate cancer called the Gleason score. They told me upfront that my Gleason score was a 6. The odds of recovery are remarkable with a score of 6. Well, when we got the pathology report back a few days after the surgery, they revised the Gleason score from a 6 to a 7, which further emphasized to my wife and me that we'd made the right decision going the surgery option. Everybody has to make the decision for himself, but this confirmed to us that it was the right thing to do to just get it out.

Starting a few days before the surgery, you go in and do all the prep and blood work and paperwork. I remember feeling a lot of apprehension. The night before the surgery was really tough. I think the biggest reason is that you know that, even if the surgery is successful, things are going to be different. The morning of the surgery, my family was with me at the hospital, but I didn't show a lot of emotion. When it comes down to a moment like that, you realize the things that are most important to you. It meant the world to have my family there with me.

I didn't see the doctor after the surgery, but when I woke up, my wife told me that the lymph nodes were clear, which was a great sign. I remember a huge sense of relief, knowing that the surgery was over and the cancer hopefully was contained. By that night I was walking down the hallway—a little shaky, but I was doing it.

That has now been four and a half years ago, and I am cancer-free. But it's still a trust walk with God, because no one knows for sure. There are markers along the way that will be great milestones to pass, like the first couple of PSA tests, the three-year mark, and then the five-year mark. If you can get through those without the PSA level starting to climb back up, it's a good thing. Yet, in the same breath, doctors will say that no one can know for sure. If the cancer recurs, it means that it got outside the prostate (which they don't believe is the case). Once the cancer is outside the prostate, there's treatment, but there is no cure. So that makes me trust. I have to trust God.

One of my favorite verses is found in Proverbs 3:5–6: "Trust in the Lord with all your heart and lean not on your own understanding; in all your ways submit to him, and he will make your paths straight" (NIV).

It came down to, number one, "God, do I trust you with my health," and then two, "God, do I trust you with making the right decision about treatment?" Because, unlike a lot of cancers, prostate cancer comes with a variety of treatments, and no one treatment is recommended above others. So it takes a lot of prayer and wisdom to say, here's the treatment I think I need to choose, and then trusting that God is going to help you make the right decision.

It's caused me to lean on him more. When you live in relationship with somebody like I live in relationship with my wife, and you have a crisis, it can do two things: It can drive you apart or push you into one another. I think my relationship with the Lord is the same; it has caused me to lean on him more and to lean in to him. I just feel closer to him. It also hasn't changed my ministry, but it's changed my capacity for empathy. Until you've walked down the road of someone looking you in the face and saying, "You have cancer," you can't know what that feels like. Now I know what it feels like, and I can better empathize with someone who's also walked that road.

We sometimes look at ourselves as though we're earthly beings having a spiritual experience every once in a while. The truth is, we're spiritual beings having a very temporary earthly experience. You have to put your trust in something far greater than even medicine and doctors. If that was all your trust is in, then it would be a pretty rough go. But thankfully there's something I can put my faith and trust and hope in that's beyond this earthly experience.

We're all going to die. The truth is we've been given a way to know that we don't have to stay this way. That's our great hope. Put your faith and hope and trust in this, not in somebody saying, "We hope we got all the cancer." You have to think a lot bigger than that and know that God has his hand in your life and is involved in what is going on in your life. **—Dan Dean**

Great I Am

Composed by Jared Anderson
Album: *Breathe* In (2012)

*God said to Moses, "I AM WHO I AM. This is what you
are to say to the Israelites: 'I AM has sent me to you.'"
(Ex. 3:14 NIV).*

I want to be close, close to Your side
So Heaven is real and death is a lie
I want to hear voices of angels above
Singing as one

Chorus:
Hallelujah, holy, holy
God Almighty, the great I AM
Who is worthy, none beside Thee
God Almighty, the great I AM

I want to be near, near to Your heart
Loving the world and hating the dark
I want to see dry bones living again
Singing as one

Chorus

The great I AM

The mountains shake before You the demons run and
flee
At the mention of the name King of Majesty
There is no power in hell
Or any who can stand
Before the power and the presence of the great I AM

The great I AM the great I AM yeah

Chorus x2

The great I AM
The great I AM
The great I AM

The Story Behind the Song

When we put together an album, each of us usually will try
our hand at writing several songs. Naturally, we all believe
our songs are the best. Then we come back to Earth as we
wrestle to decide which songs we'll include. We may write
ten songs apiece for the project, but we only include one
or two.

One of the reasons we can't include all of them is that we're always sent a bunch of great songs by writers all across the country. That was the case for this song. When we were putting together *Breathe In*, this was one of many songs we were considering.

Some songs hit you quickly. As soon as you start one, you realize right away it's a hit. Other songs grow on you slowly.

This song grew on me slowly. I remember one day listening to it as I drove in my F-150 with my wife. It starts off mellow and quiet. Then it gets to this wonderful chorus—and it just starts to grow on you. At about that point, I told my wife that there's something special about this song.

But then, as it gets to the line, "Or any who can stand / Before the power and the presence of the great I AM," it crescendos and so reflects the lyrics that it blows you away.

That's when I realized we had a hit.

I think the song's message has particular relevance for our lives today. We like to speak of God as our buddy, our great cosmic friend. Yet when the Bible describes God, it makes much of his holiness. God isn't like us. He is completely other.

This song catapults us from our ordinary, everyday world to the throne room of God, a place where demons tremble and angels echo praises of God throughout eternity because of how great God is.

I think Jared Anderson did a terrific job painting a picture of an important tension in the Christian life. On one side God wants us to know him and have personal relationship with him. Yet he is our "Great I Am," the first and the last.

He is completely worthy of our respect—and even fear.

That tension is why God is the most interesting person I've ever known. I could study him for hours every day for the rest of my life and not scratch the surface of who he is. He is our Father—but he is our holy, heavenly Father. He is grace and truth.

I'm confident that no matter who you've met in this world and what you've done, when you come face to face with this Great I Am, you're meeting the most interesting person you'll ever meet, as well. **—Shawn**

"Great I Am" is about that moment where you're just hanging out with God, but then there's this awareness that you've stepped over the threshold into the Holy of Holies—and you become aware of the spiritual world in a grander way.

We've recorded a lot of songs that talk about the majesty and greatness of God, and this is one of those. When the dust settles on everything, it's just all about him.

I think if you love Jesus and you get to the bridge, it's going to be hard for you to just sit there and yawn. That's just impossible. It gets in your soul. **—Dean Dean**

Lessons from "Great I Am"

Shawn says, "I think the song's message has particular relevance for our lives today. We like to speak of God as our buddy, our great cosmic friend. Yet when the Bible describes God, it makes much of his holiness. God isn't like us. He is completely other." What does it mean to say God is completely other?

_____

_____

_____

_____

_____

_____

_____

The Bible says, "Holy, holy, holy is the Lord God Almighty, who was, and is, and is to come... You are worthy, our Lord and God, to receive glory and honor and power, for you created all things, and by your will they were created and have their being" (Rev. 4:8, 11 NIV). This passage speaks about the majesty of God. Spend some time praising God and telling him how much he means to you, that you acknowledge he is the Lord God Almighty and no more a buddy or a cosmic friend.

_____

_____

_____

_____

_____

_____

_____

_____

_____

_____

_____

_____

_____

_____

"Jesus said to them, 'I assure you: Before Abraham was, I am'" (John 8:58 HCSB).

Great I Am: *Testimonies*

There seems to have been The Fourth Man in the Fire when they recorded this. I love worshiping God along with this song. —The Librarian

Has anyone had spiritual warfare going on you could almost feel it physically? What a great song for battle. I love this worship song and how the presence of God comes and dwells. —cinderellygirl

Rich in scriptural references, the "Great I AM" is a song that you can't do without. "The mountains shake before You. The demons run in fear at the mention of the name King of Majesty . . ." He is worthy! It can sometimes be hard to find Christian songs that are so well grounded in the Bible as this one is. It clearly points out that Jesus is the Holy One of Israel and it's his amazing grace before which we fall on our knees.

One of my favorite titles for Jesus is the Great I AM. When I was little, I didn't really understand it, but as I have grown older the depth of my understanding has increased. It expresses his Deity so well. I even had to make a bumper sticker for my car that reads: "Jesus . . . The Great I AM."

Just as he identified himself to Moses as the Everlasting God, the One who is before and above all things . . . Jesus is the Great, the only, the Almighty, the Great I AM!

I never ever get tired of hearing the name of the Lord exalted. —April

Christians know God is at the beginning, the middle, the end. And above us, below us, before us, behind us, forever and ever. The GREAT I AM is not subject to our spatial or time limitations. He is so GREAT and The I Am THAT I Am. This song illustrates how much bigger God is than we, as humans, can understand! —Brenda C

Very encouraging song about our sovereign Lord and his personal touch to impact our lives and make us more like him as he is Holy. Jesus is more than willing to make a difference in our lives and show his Glory and Love. There is none worthy beside Jesus. —Jason M

"Great I AM" is very worshipful & listening to it makes me feel God's presence & love very strongly. —Sandy J

This song is so good. It calms my soul when I am feeling anxious and puts a spring in my step when I am feeling down. —SS

When I'm feeling depressed or sad I plug this song in and praise The Great I Am and the blues go away. —justjoyce

Awesome song! Just one of those great worship songs you feel and get into! Very powerful and moving, you can't help but raise your hands high! —ChristmasAngel

This song gets me through the toughest days. When I feel alone, it connects me to the meaningfulness of living. — Yvonne T

The words of this song bring me peace in this troubled world. Reminding me that the Great I Am is with me! —Rhonda

I listen to this song every day. It reminds me of God's promises and how truly great and wonderful he is. —Poindextrous

This song brings me to tears every time I hear it. What a powerful message of the greatness of our God. —SueB

This song gives me chills!! It is now my ringtone . . . love love love love love love love love love. —tlk

This is one of the most anointed songs I have heard. Our God is the MOST HIGH GOD and the Great I AM. —ifihadwings

> "For everything was created by Him, in heaven and on earth, the visible and the invisible, whether thrones or dominions or rulers or authorities— all things have been created through Him and for Him.
>
> "He is before all things, and by Him all things hold together. He is also the head of the body, the church; He is the beginning, the firstborn from the dead, so that He might come to have first place in everything" (Col. 1:16–18 HCSB).

Tell Your Heart to Beat Again

Composed by Bernie Herms, Matthew West,
and Randy Phillips
Album: *Breathe In* (2012)

*"When you were stuck in your old sin-dead life, you
were incapable of responding to God. God brought
you alive—right along with Christ! Think of it! All sins
forgiven . . ." (Col. 2:13 The Message).*

Forgiven
If only you'd forgive yourself
You've been made new
But you're standing where you fell
Because when you look in the mirror
It seems like all you ever see
Are the scars of every failure
And the you that you used to be

Tell your heart to beat again
Close your eyes and breathe it in
Let the shadows fall away

You'll live to love another day
Yesterday's a closing door
And you don't live there anymore
So say goodbye to where you've been
And tell your heart to beat again

Forgiven
Just let that word wash over you
It's all right now
Love's healing hands have pulled you through
So, get back up and take step one
And now you're new life has begun
And know that if the Son has set you free
Then you are free indeed!

Tell your heart to beat again
Close your eyes and breathe it in
Let the shadows fall away
You'll live to love another day
Yesterday's a closing door
And you don't live there anymore
So say goodbye to where you've been
And tell your heart to beat again

Hope is reaching from a rugged cross
Where a perfect love recaptured all the innocence that's
lost
And mercy's calling from an empty grave

So lift your eyes to heaven
And hear your Savior say

Tell your heart to beat again
Close your eyes and breathe it in
Let the shadows fall away
You'll live to love another day
Yesterday's a closing door
And you don't live there anymore
So say goodbye to where you've been
And tell your heart to beat again

The Story Behind the Song

I have a pastor friend who is a real "adrenaline junkie." He'll do just about anything that involves danger and new experiences. He likes to tackle life head-on. He'll ride motorcycles, jump out of airplanes—and do whatever it takes to get the most out of life. A few years back a heart surgeon in his congregation gave him the opportunity to see an open-heart surgery firsthand.

Before the surgery started, the doctor told my friend what to expect. As far as heart surgeries are concerned, he expected it to be a fairly standard operation. The patient would come in, get prepped for surgery, and then they'd do that horrific procedure of sawing open the chest cavity. The doctor would then take the heart out of the chest, repair it, and put it back in. With just one touch by the doctor, the heart should start beating again.

Most of the surgery went as expected. The surgeon repaired the heart, massaged it, and put it back into the chest cavity. But it didn't immediately start beating. So the surgeon did it once again. No change. The surgeon tried a few other extreme measures, but nothing seemed to work.

At that point the surgeon did something incredibly unusual. He knelt down, took off his surgeon's mask, and whispered into the patient's ear: "Mrs. Johnson, this is your surgeon. Your surgery was successful. Now tell your heart to beat again."

Somewhere down in her subconscious, the patient did just that. She sent a signal to her heart, and that repaired heart began beating again.

When I heard that story, the message of this song started coming to me. There are many people whose hearts have been repaired by the Great Surgeon at great cost—the death and resurrection of his Son. Yet they're living like they're dead.

They're saved, but they're shackled by guilt and stress even though Jesus has made their heart new again.

So to anyone who's had a broken heart or has a wounded heart, the Surgeon tells you, "Tell your heart to beat again."

The truth is, Jesus has done all that's necessary for them to live again. The only thing left is for them to tell their hearts to beat again. God has done his part. Now it is time for them to do their part. **—Randy**

The energy that comes from the audience back to the stage when in concert you sing a song that they are familiar with is quite remarkable. One such song is "Tell Your Heart to Beat Again" from our last album. When people hear the back-story behind the song and then hear the song live, something really remarkable always happens with that song in particular. On some occasions, it's as if I can actually see hope coming to a heart, right in the moment. **—Dan**

Lessons from "Tell Your Heart to Beat Again"

The Bible says, "He died for us, a death that triggered life. Whether we're awake with the living or asleep with the dead, we're alive with him!" (1 Thess. 5:10 *The Message*). How does the death of Christ bring life to us?

_____

_____

_____

_____

_____

The song lyrics say, "Yesterday's a closing door And you don't live there anymore. So say goodbye to where you've been And tell your heart to beat again." What ways have you tried to live in the past? Why does God want you to close the door and move forward?

_____

_____

_____

_____

_____

_____

_____

The song lyrics say, "Forgiven. Just let that word wash over you. It's all right now Love's healing hands have pulled you through." Why is understanding that you're forgiven so essential to being healed?

_____

_____

_____

_____

_____

_____

_____

_____

> "But because of his great love for us, God, who is rich
> in mercy, made us alive with Christ even when we
> were dead in transgressions—it is by grace you have
> been saved" (Eph. 2:4–5 NIV).

Tell Your Heart to Beat Again:
Testimonies

I just wanted to share how this song has ministered to me for many months now, and has been one of many tools in giving me courage to go forward. My husband died in January 2015. When that happens, oftentimes though you keep going on everyday things (working, cleaning, eating, etc.) it's scary to know how to do other things alone when all your plans and conversations and hopes and tasks have been tied to that person.

In the last few months, I left my job, home, car, friends, and surroundings to move from Arizona to Minnesota to be near our children. It's been wonderful, but on days when even going to the grocery store by myself has taken courage and brought so many memories of past happiness, the words "say goodbye to where you've been and tell your heart to beat again . . . you don't live there anymore" have been a gentle reminder and strengthener to turn my face and thoughts and actions forward—and walk a new walk with hope and much joy! —JS

WOW!!! There is NOTHING like telling it like it really is!!! I have loved P C & D as long as I have known of them. Their songs helped when the unimaginably horrible happened to some precious young people who went to school with our children. —HeHumbled

"Tell Your Heart to Beat Again" was shared with me at a time in my life where I did not realize that I was not really living but just surviving. As it played, I actually felt the words speak life and my heart start beating. —Karen O

Beautiful & meaningful lyrics. This song speaks heartfelt truths of God and His great love for each of us; His creation. —Patricia S

If you realize who you are, and Who He IS, and you look at any error in your life's timeline . . . this song speaks it all. This one always gets me. —Fredrick M

Salvation Is Free

Everybody has to go to the cross if you're going to follow Christ. The Lord said, "Take up your cross and follow me." Taking up the cross means to let go of who you think you are and embrace who he says you are. I am not my own—I'm his. Everyday I have to make the choice to follow him. I make decisions on a daily basis that I probably wouldn't make if I didn't have a cross on my shoulder. I make a different decision because I go to the cross.

Through the resurrection, we realize that whatever has died in my life can come back to life because of what Jesus did in that tomb—conquering death, Hell, and the grave. There is nothing that can't be overcome because of the power of the resurrection. **—Randy**

The path toward spiritual freedom will take you beyond self-reliance and DIY religion. God's commands will push you beyond your natural ability. Its purpose is to leave you exhausted on the floor from the rat race of self-effort and independence until you are panting and helpless between a rock and a hard place—until all you can do is to cry out, "Who will free me from this life that is dominated by sin and death?" (Rom. 7:24). **—Shawn Craig**

I spent thirty-plus years of my life trying to get good so that God would love me. Part of the revelation came through a friend of mine that I heard sharing a sermon called "No Sweat." He mentioned that "sweat" occurs three times in the Bible. One is associated with the curse, where part of the curse was, "You're going to sweat." The third time that everybody's familiar with is Jesus's sweat as if it were great drops of blood. And then the middle mention of the word "sweat" is instructions given to the high priests when they were to go in to minister before the Lord. It's a little known scripture in Ezekiel 44:18 that says that when they go into the Holy Place, "they shall not bind themselves with anything that causes sweat" (ESV).

The message was that it's an affront to God to go into his presence thinking we can do anything that represents work. There's nothing we can do to earn his grace or his goodness. The day that that dawned on me—that I don't have to work, that he loves me regardless, that all I have to do is accept the gift—it was the most freeing, defining moment.

Somebody reading these words is no doubt going through the same thing. When I grew up, it was the doctrine of eternal insecurity. I felt like I had to get saved every Sunday at church because during the week I had fallen short. But God loves me enough, he provides me the gift of salvation, and I don't have to do anything to deserve it. I just have to receive it. To come to that realization is an incredible moment in anybody's life. **—Dan Dean**

I pray that before you give in to that haunting temptation or to the weight of despair, or you give up on prayer or the promises of God, you'll go back and stand before the cross a bit. Visit the tomb. Read about the people in Scripture who had given up. I pray you'll take a look at the disciples who morphed from fearful cowards to emboldened witnesses after the resurrection of Jesus.

So when you find yourself in one of those moments, stand in front of the Empty Tomb. Remind yourself that God the Father must really love you. Our prayer is that love would rise above whatever might want to sink your ship.

The Empty Tomb is the only anchor we need. Nothing can ever change that—not politics, not ISIS, not terror. Nothing can separate us from the love of God. John Piper says, "Grace is power, not just pardon."

Grace empowers us in the gospel. It empowers us to live above sin. It empowers us in our darkness.

At the end of the day, grace isn't just pardon, it's power to live through our darkest day. Our hope is that through our songs you'll be reminded of that gospel. —**Shawn**

Thank You for Twenty-Five Years of Trust

If there's anything we've tried to communicate as a group, it is that God loves his children. Whether it's "Mercy Came Running," "He'll Do Whatever It Takes," or numerous other songs, the grace of God has been a theme of our ministry. One time when we were trying out a new song about grace, my wife asked, "Haven't you guys about covered that topic?" But it's a subject you can't exhaust. It's too big and too broad for us ever to run out of ways to sing about it. **—Dan**

We want people to love Jesus more. Whatever view you have of Jesus—whether your relationship is vibrant or stale—our prayer is that when you hear our songs, you'll feel the Holy Spirit dancing through every line. Our prayer for whoever engages our music is that they would open their hearts one more time to Jesus and give him another chance. **—Randy**

We think the group will continue to sing as long as God gives us strength to do that and we're all healthy. Every time we think we're about through with the touring and the recording thing, God shows up in some really crazy way." **—Randy, Shawn, & Dan**

Favorite Songs by Album

Phillips, Craig & Dean (1992)
- Turn Up the Radio
- Little Bit of Morning
- Midnight Oil
- Favorite Song of All

Lifeline (1994)
- He'll Do Whatever It Takes
- Build a Bridge of Love
- I Want to Be Just Like You
- Concert of the Age

GMA Dove Nomination—Inspirational Album of the Year, 1995

Trust (1995)
- Mercy Came Running
- Crucified with Christ

My Utmost for His Highest—Artist Compilation (1995)

- Shine On Us

GMA Dove Award—Special Event Album of the Year, 1995

Where Strength Begins (1997)
- New Mercy
- Where Strength Begins
- Blessing in the Thorn
- Just One

- This Is How It Feels to Be Free

Restoration (1999)
- I've Got You Covered

Let My Words Be Few (2001)
- Let My Words Be Few

Fearless (2009)
- Revelation Song
- Great Are You Lord

GMA Dove Award—Inspirational Album of the Year, 2010

Breathe In (2012)
- When the Stars Burn Down
- Great, Great God
- Great I Am
- Tell Your Heart To Beat Again

Above It All (2014)
- Jesus, Only Jesus

Phillips, Craig & Dean

Discography:
- *Hymns* (2016)
- *Breathe In* (2012)
- *Hope for All the World* (2010)
- *Fearless* (2009)

- *Top of My Lungs* (2006)
- *Let the Worshippers Arise* (2004)
- *Let Your Glory Fall* (2003)
- *Let My Words Be Few* (2001)
- *Restoration* (1999)
- *Favorite Songs of All* (1998)
- *Where Strength Begins* (1997)
- *Repeat the Sounding Joy* (1996)
- *Trust* (1995)
- *Lifeline* (1993)
- *Phillips, Craig & Dean* (1992)

Awards and Recognition:

- 2015 Dove Award for "Inspiration Album of the Year"—*Above It All*
- 2010 Dove Award for "Inspiration Album of the Year"—*Fearless*
- 2006 Favorite Inspirational Artist—*CCM Magazine* Reader's Choice
- 2005 Favorite Inspirational Artist—*CCM Magazine* Reader's Choice
- 2000 CCM's Inspirational Song of the Decade (90s) for "Crucified With Christ"
- 1996 Dove Award for "Special Event Album of the Year"—*My Utmost For His Highest*
- 1993 CCM #1 Song of the Year, "Favorite Song of All"
- 1993 CRR Reader's Poll #2 favorite group

- 1992 *Christian Research Report's* New Artist of the Year

Nominations:
- 2007 Dove Award nomination for "Praise & Worship Album"
- 2005 Dove Award nomination for "Praise & Worship Album"
- 1997 Dove Award nomination for Song of the Year, "Crucified With Christ"
- 1997 Dove Award nomination for Inspirational Song of the Year, "Crucified With Christ"
- 1995 Dove Award nomination for Inspirational Album of the Year, *Lifeline*
- 1995 Dove Award nomination for Inspirational Song of the Year, "I Want To Be Just Like You"
- 1994 American Christian Music Awards, Favorite Pop Group
- 1993 Dove Award nomination for Best New Artist

Radio:
- "You Are God Alone"
- "Friend of God," No. 2 on AC ,Top AC & INSPO
- "Your Name," "Saved the Day," and "Top of My Lungs" all landed Top 5 spots on the INSPO chart
- TWENTY ONE No. 1 songs including favorites such as "Let My Words Be Few," "Great Are You

Lord," and "Revelation Song," which was also No. 1 at INSPO for eighteen weeks in a row.

Additional facts:

- 25 years of ministry as Phillips, Craig & Dean
- 14 albums
- 21 No. 1 singles
- 3 million records sold
- Each band member is also a full-time pastor at their respective churches
- Phillips, Craig & Deans' "Saved the Day" from their 2006 INO Records' release "Top of My Lungs" is played in front of nearly 25,000 people as Texas Rangers' outfielder Josh Hamilton enters the Rangers Ballpark in Arlington, Texas

Author Bio Sketches

Randy Phillips

- Pastor of LifeAustin Church in Austin, Texas.
- Host of "The Awakening," a long-running worship series—taped in Austin and has aired nationally on TBN and other channels.
- Wife: Denise; children: Garland and Lily.

Shawn Craig

- Pastor of Crosspoint Church in St. Louis, Missouri.

- Masters of Divinity at Oral Roberts University in Tulsa, Oklahoma.
- Won three GMA Dove Awards for the song "In Christ Alone" (1993—Inspirational Recorded Song of the Year;1994—Song of the Year; 2006—Inspirational Recorded Song of the Year again).
- Wife: Becki Craig née Trueblood is a member of Heritage Singers.

Dan Dean

- Pastor of The Heartland Church in Carrollton, Texas. Just celebrated thirty-one years of being part of the staff with the last sixteen a lead pastor.
- Began (like Craig) as music/worship director before becoming senior pastor.
- Wife: Becky; children: Dusty, Devin, and Danielle; daughters-in-law: Kendra. and Kendell; son-in-law: Nick; grandchildren: Sailor, Jayden, Liam, and Brooklyn.